THE   COTTON   CLUB


Screenplay by:

WILLIAM KENNEDY & FRANCIS COPPOLA

Story by:

WILLIAM KENNEDY & FRANCIS COPPOLA
          AND MARIO PUZO


FINAL SCRIPT

December 8, 1983

THE COTTON CLUB. Copyright © 1986 by Totally Independent, Ltd. All rights reserved. Printed in the United States of America. No part of this book may be used or reproduced in any manner whatsoever without written permission except in the case of brief quotations embodied in critical articles or reviews. For information, address St. Martin's Press, 175 Fifth Avenue, New York, N.Y. 10010.

Library of Congress Cataloging in Publication Data

Coppola, Francis Ford, 1939-
  Cotton Club.

  I. Kennedy, William, 1928-    .  II. Cotton Club
(Motion picture: 1984)   III. Title.
PN1997.C833   1986        791.43′72        86-6485
ISBN 0-312-17017-3 (pbk.)

First U.S. Edition

10 9 8 7 6 5 4 3 2 1

## CAST OF CHARACTERS

DALBERT "SANDMAN" WILLIAMS
Numbers runner,
aspiring dancer.

LILA ROSE OLIVER
Cotton Club showgirl
and singer.

MADAME ST. CLAIR
Numbers queen. Late 30's.

BUMPY RHODES
Harlem gangster.

CLAY WILLIAMS
Sandman's brother
and dancing partner.

NORMA WILLIAMS
Sandman's mother.

WINNER WILLIAMS
Sandman's younger
sister.

SUGAR COATS
President of Hoofers
Club. Sandman's friend.

BUB JEWETT
Harlem gangster.

CASPAR HOLSTEIN
ALEXANDER POMPEZ
BIG JOE ISON
MARCIAL FLORES
SPANISH HENRY
Harlem numbers
bankers.

KID GRIFFIN
Suave maitre d'.

MICHAEL "DIXIE" DWYER
Aspiring musician, dancer,
show business guy.

DUTCH SCHULTZ
Big time gangster.
Young, ambitious, cruel.

VERA CICERO
Dutch's beautiful
showgirl paramour.

OWEN MADDEN
Owner of Cotton Club.
Elder statesman mobster.

FRENCHY DEMANGE
Racketeer. Boss
around the club.

VINCENT DWYER
Dixie's younger brother.
Berserk punk.

TISH DWYER
DIxie's mother.

PATSY DWYER
Vincent's wife. Young
'cupcake'.

ABBADABBA BERMAN
Associate of Dutch.
Mathematical genius.

SOL WEINSTEIN
Dutch's aide. Big, old
and lethal.

FRANCES FLEGENHEIMER
Dutch's wife. Straight-
laced ex-hat check girl.

HOLMES
The doorman;
an ex-fighter.

ELIDA WEBB
Choreographer.

JOE
Custodian of club.

RUBY
Chorus girl.

ETHEL
Chorus girl.

DUKE ELLINGTON
Bandleader.

CAB CALLOWAY
Bandleader.

THE MESSIAH
Harlem character.

MACRUS GARVEY
Black nationalist.

MIKE BEST
Meanest and toughest
club bruiser.

HERMAN STARK
Club manager.

TED HUSING
Radio broadcaster.

ED POPKE
Vince's best friend.

JOE FLYNN
Gangster rival of Dutch.

CHARLES "LUCKY" LUCIANO
Big time gangster.

MONK
Madden's bodyguard, driver.

GLORIA SWANSON
Famous actress.

CHARLIE CHAPLIN
Famous actor.


SINGERS, DANCERS, MUSICIANS, GANGSTERS,
AND THE HOI POLLOI.



PLACE:   HARLEM

TIME:   THE JAZZ AGE

## MUSICAL NUMBERS

Am I Blue
Bandanna Babies
Barbecue Bess
Between the Devil & the Deep Blue Sea
Breakin' in a New Pair of Shoes
Bugle Call Rag
Butter and Egg Man
Copper Colored Gal
Crazy Rhythm
Creole Love Call
Creole Rhapsody
Daybreak Express
Diga Diga Do
Doin' the New Low Down
Don't Let the Blues go to Your Feet
Go Back Where You Stayed Last Night
Hoofers Club Dance
Ill Wind
It Don't Mean a Thing
Jitterbug
Lady Be Good
Lady With the Fan
Minnie the Moocher
Mooche
Nicholas Brothers
One Man Dance
Pah Pah Dee Dah Dah
Shake that Thing
Skrontch
Stormy Weather
Tall, Tan, Terrific
Them There Eyes
Tip, Tap, Toe
Truckin'
White Heat

FADE IN:

1   EXT - HARLEM - DAY:   <u>HARLEM HISTORY MONTAGE</u>

Original arrangement of "Mood Indigo."  The MAIN TITLE and CREDITS begin.

INSERT: street sign - "Lenox & 142nd street."  (1905-1915)

VIEW of a Harlem boulevard, a white neighborhood.  Horses, buggies (new), delivery wagon, bicycles.  Families walk greeting each other.  Children play in street.

INSERT: "For Sale" and "Rent" signs -- "Desirable Apartments for Desirable Colored Tenants."  Opportunity shops with "help wanted" signs.  Posters, news ads.

Blacks begin to occupy the houses and apartments.

Soldiers with guns, perfect, with pride.  The "Harlem Hellfighters", returning from the war.  People crowd around cheering, waving flags.

Crowds of blacks on street corner.  Banners of "Back to Africa".  Marcus Garvey steps out of limo in uniform.

INSERT: street sign (new) "Lenox & 142nd street."  (1929)

Cars and cycles driven by blacks.  Black cop.  Black children play in street.  Posters and ads.  Black families greet each other.  Black children tap dance for money.

Numbers runners take bets from old people, kids.  Stacks of change.  BUMPY RHODES, MADAME ST. CLAIR supervise six men checking numbers slips, runners paying off bets.

<u>NIGHT FALLS</u>.

Black night clubs, social clubs, jazz joints, dance halls are abundant.  Raucous JAZZ MUSIC here.

Feet step up curb, booze breaks.  People enter "Tillie's Chicken House", speakeasy, get past bouncer.  Smoke filled room.  Men picking up on women.  Smoke trails up woman's leg.  Back room crap game.  Girls taking drugs.

INSERT: blinking signs, racing lights.  Woman's dress drops to her ankles.  Seltzer bottle squirts.  THE MESSIAH, a tattered Harlem prophet, walks down the street, barefoot.

MESSIAH
...The wages of sin is death!

2  EXT - COTTON CLUB - NIGHT:  <u>DIXIE POV COTTON CLUB</u>

Lenox & 142nd: MICHAEL "DIXIE" DWYER approaches Cotton Club, a silhouette and shadow carrying cornet case, clothing bag.

DIXIE'S POV:

People in evening clothes are getting out of taxis and limousines. The poor negro residents gather to gawk from a distance. The taxi drivers are fighting for space on the line for the Cotton Club. Two CABBIES jockeying for a spot in line. Dixie's shadow shakes his head affectionately.

> DIXIE
> Harlem, sweet Harlem,
> I got your number.

The black doorman, HOLMES, a tall and powerful ex-fighter, is letting most people pass, but stops a couple and looks carefully at the WOMAN, who is dark haired and dark complexioned, and the MAN, blond and rich.

CLOSE ON HOLMES

Grim and serious, as Dixie watches.

> HOLMES
> This lady look like a colored
> lady to me.

> MAN
> She's nothing of the sort.
> She's white. Pure Spanish
> blood.

> WOMAN
> I was born in Barcelona.

> HOLMES
> Don't they have no colored
> folk over there in Barcelona?

> MAN
> This is most insulting.
> I want to see the manager.

CLOSE ON DIXIE

Coming out of the shadows, chuckling to himself.

                    DIXIE
          Lenox Avenue, you're a bear.
          Chocolate Harlem!


19   EXT - LENOX AVENUE - NIGHT:   <u>SANDMAN ON NUMBERS BEAT</u>

     CLOSE ON SANDMAN WILLIAMS, moving like a dancer, on his beat
     to pick up numbers. He goes in and out of stores, stops on
     front stoops to talk to people.

                    SANDMAN
          Hey, Mo, whataya like today?

                    MO
          Thanksgivin's comin', so
          they say. 527 always comes
          up Thanksgivin'.

     At the next store, to a buxom middle-aged woman.

                    SANDMAN
               (winking)
          I want your business, Ada.

     Ada gives him the money as he writes the last number.

                    ADA
          5-2-7 honey, and you give
          me a call.


2A   EXT - COTTON CLUB - NIGHT:   <u>SANDMAN PAYS OFF DIXIE</u>

     People getting out of a car catch Holmes' attention. This
     is JACK "LEGS" DIAMOND and gorgeous brunette, preceded and
     followed by two THUGS.

                    HOLMES
          Welcome to the Cotton Club,
          Mr. Legs Diamond...

                    DIAMOND
          Keep punchin', Holmes.

     The gangster and his group pass into the club. Dixie's
     impressed. Holmes sees Dixie.

                    HOLMES
          Hey, Dixie, greatest music in
          the world upstairs. You gonna
          give a listen? I'll let you
          stand in the hallway.

                    DIXIE
          Goin' down the street and play
          my own music, Holmes.  How come
          you're hustlin' for the ofays?

                    HOLMES
          The fay pays, man.  Who you
          workin' for?  Heard you was
          on the road.

                    DIXIE
          Band fell apart in Chicago and
          I come home on a bus, pinin'
          for the sound of Harlem.

Sandman walks by.  Holmes buys a number.

                    SANDMAN
          Hey, what is it today with
          the Thanksgiving number?  Five-
          two is seven, seven come seven.
          Everybody cravin' turkey.

                    HOLMES
          That number come up three years
          in a row on Thanksgivin'.

                    SANDMAN
          Hey Dixie, where you been?
          I owe you money for six weeks.

Sandman takes out roll of bills and gives Dixie $120.

                    DIXIE
          I hit?

Dixie opens cornet case and puts money inside, and the two head for the Bamville Club.

                    DIXIE
          How's your numbers career,
          Sandman?

                    SANDMAN
          Hell, that ain't my career.

3    EXT/INT - BAMVILLE CLUB - NIGHT:  <u>BAMVILLE BOMB</u>

Dixie playing cornet in jam session, only white in band. CAMERA FINDS white customers among mostly black crowd. Sandman with other blacks, including his brother CLAY.

A distance away is the notorious black gangster, BUMPY
RHODES, standing by the bar with three tough-looking
companions. A distance away, going through the cash
register, by herself, is MADAME ST. CLAIR, also a gangster.

VIEW ON A JAZZ FAN, DUTCH SCHULTZ

Leaning forward, interested. He's sitting with two men,
ABBADABBA BERMAN, and a SULLEN MAN.

VIEW ON BAND -- Playing up-tempo tune.

VIEW ON SANDMAN AND CLAY

Dancing with some women.

Dixie gets into a duel of eight-bar solos with another horn
player. Both horn players are good, but Dixie wins. Dixie
moves away from band. As he passes table with three men
Dutch stops him.

                DUTCH
    Hey, buddy, you play nice
    horn. Buy you a drink?

Dixie eyes Vera, but sits with Dutch. Clay, Sandman leave.

                DUTCH
    That trumpet guy, you beat him
    bad. He oughta be put away for
    larceny. All those riffs, he
    just lifted 'em from King Oliver.

              ABBADABBA
    I lost a grand on a horse named
    Gideon's Trumpet. Your name
    Gideon?

                DIXIE
No.

              ABBADABBA
    Good. That jockey could hold an
    elephant away from a bale of hay
    with a pair of shoestrings.

                DUTCH
    For chrissake, Abbadabba, the
    man's a musician, not a jockey.
    (to Dixie) But do you make a
    livin' with that horn?

                    DIXIE
          I'm eatin' but I'm not gettin'
          fat.  I play a little piano,
          too.  You heard Oliver play?

                    DUTCH
          I caught him at the Savoy.

Dutch looks toward women with lustful eye.  SOL WEINSTEIN is
a distance away, watches over Dutch like a mother.

                    DIXIE
               (to the girls)
          Hey, whataya sittin' over there
          for?  Come on over here so we
          can take your breath away.

The girls laugh among themselves, pick up their drinks, come
over.  Dixie stands up and Dutch stares in disbelief.  Vera
and Myrtle arrive, giggling.

                    VERA
               (to Dixie)
          What'll I sit on?  Wait a
          minute.  Don't answer that.

                    DIXIE
          Just don't sit on the best
          part of your personality.

                    ABBADABBA
          Let me guess your names.

                    MYRTLE
          It's Myrtle and no cracks.

                    VERA
          Vera, as in very very.
          Cicero, as in Latin.
          You ever study Latin?

                    DIXIE
          I was an altar boy.

VIEW ON THE DOORWAY

TWO POLICEMEN enter, walk slowly, without obvious purpose,
toward center of club.

                    VERA
               (handles Dixie's tie)
          That's a lovely necktie.
               (handles Dutch's tie)
          Your tie stinks.

                    DUTCH
               (smiles widely)
          But I got nice teeth.  And a
          lot of money.  (flashes roll
          of bills)

                    DIXIE
          Well, how do you like
          us so far?

Vera sits down and spills her drink on Abbadabba who backs
up and tips table, knocking two drinks into lap of Dutch.
Dixie and the others are trying to sort out the confusion of
the spilled drink.  One policeman proves to have a pistol in
his hand, the other one has a small, homemade bomb and rolls
it at Dixie's table.  The girls, not yet seated, scream and
fall behind the next table.

Abbadabba falls toward girls.  Dutch is grazed by pistol
shot from exiting cop, Dixie hits Dutch with flying block;
they are behind table when the grenade goes off.  The sullen
man gets the brunt of the explosion, and his arm is badly
ripped.  All this has taken place in a few seconds.  Dutch
has a pistol in his fist now but nothing to shoot at.

                    DIXIE
          What the hell was that all
          about?

                    DUTCH
          Some people don't like me.

                    DIXIE
          Who are you?

                    DUTCH
               (sincerely)
          I'm your Dutch uncle from now
          on, pal.  I owe you a big one.

The sullen man's arm is dangling.  Abbadabba is down but
only winged, and looking up Myrtle's dress.  Both girls are
sprawled on the floor in terror.

                    DIXIE
          You all right?

                    VERA
          Pow!  They do that every
          night here?

                    DIXIE
          If you're lucky.  You wanna
          go home?

                    VERA
          I'm very swoozled.  I think
          I should.

                    DIXIE
          Do you want to go to the
          hospital for your brains?

                    VERA
          I want to go home.

5     INT - VERA'S APARTMENT - NIGHT:   DIXIE PUTS VERA TO BED

The two enter, Vera finds light, Dixie leads her to sofa and
lowers her gently.  She half collapses, but is awake.  He
helps her to bed, helps her take off her skirt and blouse,
leaving her in her slip.  He's keeping arm's length.

                    DIXIE
          Get under the covers.

                    VERA
          I can't sleep with this harness.

She tries to undo bra, can't manage it.  He helps her, then
makes sure her slip straps go back where they belong.

                    DIXIE
          You do the stockings.

                    VERA
          Quit being an altar boy and
          give a little girl a hand.

Dixie undoes second garter, helps her peel off stockings,
unsnaps and pulls off garter belt, rolls her into bed.

                    VERA
          Hey.  I liked the way you
          played your trumpet.  You
          sounded like Gabriel.

                    DIXIE
          It's a cornet.  Gabriel
          plays the sax.

                    VERA
          Whatever it is, don't go home
          with it and leave me alone.

Dixie nods and puts out light. He reconnoiters, finds a pillow, lies on couch, falls asleep.

DISSOLVE:

6   INT - SANDMAN'S BEDROOM - DAY: <u>SANDMAN WAKES UP</u>

Sandman wakes up. His brother Clay is still asleep.

              SANDMAN
      Hey, Clay, wake up...

              CLAY
      Shhh. Don't make noise.

              SANDMAN
      The audition...

Clay wakes up with a start.

7   INT - WILLIAMS APARTMENT - DAY: <u>WILLIAMS' DISCUSS BOMB</u>

FOLLOW SANDMAN to kitchen, where he sits with coffee and toast. His mother, NORMA, is reading the paper.

              NORMA
      Didn't you say you were at
      the Bamville last night?

              SANDMAN
      Yeah. Why?

              NORMA
      How come you didn't say nothin'
      about that bomb?

              SANDMAN
      What bomb you talkin' about?

              NORMA
      Dalbert, they throw a bomb at
      you and blow off a man's arm
      and you still doing the soft
      shoe?

              SANDMAN
          (looking at the paper)
      I was gone.

              NORMA
      Them bums. They're just bums,
      blow a man's arm off like that.

Clay enters.

                    CLAY
          Whose arm got blown off?

                    NORMA
          You didn't hear the bomb either?

INSERT:  Headline plus photos of Schultz and Flynn brothers.

          "THREE WOUNDED IN CLUB SHOOTOUT"
         "Dutch Schultz Target of Flynn Brothers"

                    SANDMAN o.s.
                (reads)
          "...Police said the Bamville
          bombing was another skirmish in
          the beer war between Dutch
          Schultz and...."

8   INT - LUNCHEONETTE - DAY:  <u>DIXIE/VINCE DISCUSS BOMB</u>

VINCE DWYER passes the same article to his brother Dixie, who is eating ham and eggs.

                    VINCE
                (reading)
          ...the Flynn brothers for control
          of Harlem beer distribution.
                (to Dixie)  Where were you?
          You saw the bomb coming.

                    DIXIE
          With Schultz.  I saved his
          ass.  Shoved him down behind
          a table.

                    VINCE
          You saved the Dutchman's ass?
          No kiddin'?

They exit.

9   EXT - STREET - DAY:  <u>DUTCH NEEDS APES</u>

MOVING SHOT on Vince and Dixie walking.

                    VINCE
          Listen, think about it.  You
          saved the Dutchman means that
          the Dwyer brothers are in.

                    DIXIE
          In where, you sap?

VIEW ON ED POPKE

He's crossing the street, having seen Vince and Dixie. He is a small shifty-eyed young hoodlum, not well-dressed.

                    ED
          Wait up, Vince. (to Dixie)
          Hey, you're some big time hero.
          The Dutchman's tellin' people
          you saved his life.

                    VINCE
          Get in line. I got rakes on
          that Dutchman.

                    DIXIE
          What the hell is it, you two
          wantin' to work for a
          bootlegger?

                    VINCE
          Hey, he needs guys like us.
          We don't grow on trees.

                    DIXIE
          Nah, you swing from 'em, you
          ape.

10  INT - WILLIAMS APARTMENT - DAY:  <u>WINNIE PRACTICES STEP</u>

WINNIE WILLIAMS, 15, comes into breakfast, sulking.

                    SANDMAN
          Let me see your combination,
          Win.

                    WINNIE
          It's awful, I hate it.

                    NORMA
          You don't hate it. You love
          it. It's gonna make you win
          that contest.

                    SANDMAN
          You gonna do it?

She does it.

                    SANDMAN
          You still rushin'.  The
          time's not right.

                    NORMA
          Do it nice, girl, practice
          if you wanna get to the
          Cotton Club.  Let me show
          you.

Norma demonstrates how Cotton Club "showgirl" moves.

                    WINNIE
          I'm not yella enough to ever
          be a Cotton Club girl.

Clay and Sandman exit.

11-12 EXT - HARLEM STREET - DAY:   <u>BROTHERS CROSS</u>

Sandman and Clay walking down the street.

                    SANDMAN
          We got to make our audition
          number stronger.  The fays in
          the Cotton Club know what
          they're lookin' for.

                    CLAY
          What does 'stronger' mean?

                    SANDMAN
          Those white folks gonna look
          us over, they want excitement.

                    CLAY
          Sandman, you try giving white
          folks what you think they
          want pretty soon you got no
          blood left.

                    SANDMAN
          What are we gonna do?  We
          gonna do the soft shoe or
          the Ultima?

Sandman and Clay continuing conversation along sidewalk.
They and Dwyer brothers and Ed Popke cross paths.  Dixie and
Sandman greet one another with an offhand gesture.

13  EXT - DWYER APARTMENT - DAY:   <u>VINCE SAYS HE'S MARRIED</u>

   Steps to Dwyer apartment; Popke, Vince, Dixie arrive.

                    VINCE
               Listen.  Big news.  I didn't
               tell you yet.  (pause)  I
               suddenly... got married.

                    DIXIE
               What?  When... who to?

   Dixie slaps Vince on the shoulder, hard, but playfully.

                    DIXIE
               You tell me you want a job
               with Schultz but you don't
               mention you got hitched?
               What the hell ails you?

   Dixie turns to Popke.

                    DIXIE
               Do me a favor, will you,
               Popke.  Let me have a little
               privacy with the family?
               I been away six months.
               Look him up later.

   Popke reluctantly takes his leave.  Brothers climb stairs.

14-16  INT - DWYER APT - DAY:   <u>TISH WELCOMES DIXIE HOME</u>

   Vince introduces PATSY in kimono, very little underneath.

                    VINCE
               This is her, Dix.  Patsy, this
               is my big brother.

   LETITIA "TISH" DWYER teaches waltz to Harold, 9-year old
   kid.  Victrola plays a pop waltz.

                    TISH
               That's it, Harold, slide on
               the balls of your feet, one-
               two-three, one-two-three.

   Harold is dancing as if his shoes were glued to the rug.
   Vince enters, and opens curtain, revealing Dixie.

                    DIXIE
          Whataya say, Tish.  How's
          them dancin' feet?

                    TISH
          Michael, I oughta punch you
          right in the nose.  You were
          in town all day yesterday and
          you didn't even call.

                    DIXIE
          It's a long story.  Don't scold
          your wandering boy.  Throw your
          arms around me.

Tish lets go of Harold, hugs Dixie.  She turns to Harold.

                    TISH
          That'll be all for today,
          Harold.  Practice sliding,
          remember what I told you.

Harold gives her a quarter for his lesson, goes out.

                    VINCE
          Hey, Ma, Dixie was in the
          Bamville last night when they
          bombed it.

                    TISH
               (upset)
          Were you hurt?

Dixie shakes his head.  Vince jumps in before he can answer.

                    VINCE
          He shoved Dutch Schultz out
          of the way of the bomb.  He
          saved his life.

                    TISH
          Why did you do a thing like
          that?  He's a perfectly awful
          man.

                    DIXIE
          How did I know who he was?

                    TISH
          Patsy, go put some clothes on.

Patsy pouts, turns to Vince, warps herself around him.
Vince pushes Patsy down the hallway into bedroom.

                    TISH
          You save any money from your
          band tour?

Dixie reaches in pocket, pulls out wad of money and plops it
on table.  Tish riffles through it.

                    DIXIE
          I hit the number before I left
          town and didn't know it.
          Sandman paid me off last night.

                    TISH
          So you didn't save anything.

                    DIXIE
          I got some new clothes.

                    TISH
          Michael, are you ever going to
          make sense out of your life?

                    DIXIE
          What if I went in the movies?

                    TISH
          A movie actor?

                    DIXIE
          I know a guy's workin' in
          movies.  He likes my style.

                    TISH
          If you're gonna be in movies
          you've got to be a big spender.
          I want to go out on the town.

She puts on his hat and dances with him.

                    DIXIE
          You want to invite Vince and
          blushing bride?

We HEAR the wall banging as Vince and Patsy make love.

                    TISH
          Why not?  Don't you love
          the way they converse...
               (she listens)
          Just listen to her repartee.

Wall banging goes on.  Then it stops.

CLOSE ON DIXIE

Looking into their room.  He closes door.

17  EXT - COTTON CLUB - DAY:    <u>EXIT AUDITION/SEE LILA ROSE</u>

The Williams Brothers, Clay and Sandman, are coming down the steps.  At the foot of the steps, sweeping the sidewalk, is Holmes, the doorman, in everyday clothes.

     HOLMES
  You boys thinkin' you made
  it into the big time up
  there today?

     SANDMAN
  They loved us, Holmes.

     HOLMES
  Quit runnin' numbers now.
  Big money here we come.

     CLAY
  We'll see.  He was showin'
  off again.

Clay walks off without a goodbye.  Sandman gives him a screw-you gesture.  Sandman sees LILA ROSE coming toward club.  She is so beautiful that he runs to her.

     SANDMAN
  Can you help me, I'm having
  a heart attack.

     LILA ROSE
  You look real sick, all
  right.

She keeps walking.  Sandman watches her go, awed.

     HOLMES
    (amused)
  You fell off the edge, Sandman.

     SANDMAN
  I'm climbin' back on.

He runs upstairs after her.

18   INT - STAIRS - DAY:   SANDMAN/STARK ON STAIRS

At top of steps he encounters HERMAN STARK, club manager. Stark's presence stops him, and wistfully Sandman watches Lila Rose go backstage.

            SANDMAN
        Oh, Mr. Stark, sir.  I couldn't
        wait.  Do we get the job or don't
        we?

            STARK
          (grimly)
        Everybody liked you.  You'll
        go in the next show.

            SANDMAN
        You white folks are so smart.

19A  INT - COTTON CLUB - DAY:   SANDMAN WATCHES GIRLS REHEARSAL

ELIDA WEBB, the choreographer, is running girls through their paces.  Piano is rolled onto stage; Sandman approaches.

HIS POV:

Lila Rose in rehearsal with the company.  He moves around, closer.  A big hood, MIKE BEST, approaches him.

            BEST
        What do you want?

            SANDMAN
        Oh, I'm with the company.
        Mr. Stark and I...

            BEST
        I don't care what Mr. Stark
        says.  You don't use that
        front door.  You use the back
        door.

He throws him out.

21   INT - JAZZ SPEAKEASY - NIGHT:   SOL APPROACHES DIXIE

JAM SESSION -- piano, trombone, clarinet, trumpet and drums. Real jazz.

DIXIE'S POV:

A strange man sitting at the bar is looking at him.

VIEW ON DIXIE

The jam session. Sol Weinstein approaches him.

> SOL
> You're Dixie Dwyer?

> DIXIE
> That's right.

> SOL
> The Dutchman's got a job
> for you. He says you
> play the piano in addition
> to that bugle. Is that right?

> DIXIE
> Yeah, that's right.

> SOL
> He wants you to play at a
> party.

> DIXIE
> For how much?

> SOL
> A hundred and fifty.

> DIXIE
> That's a lot for some piano
> playing.

> SOL
> He owes you one.

> DIXIE
> When does he want to pay?

> SOL
> Right now.

Dixie considers the offer, nods okay.

A22 EXT - CAR - NIGHT: <u>CAR DRIVES BY</u>

Mysterious car drives by.

22  INT - CAR - NIGHT:   DIXIE/SOL DRIVE TO HOTEL

   Dixie and Weinstein in car.

                    DIXIE
              What do they call you?

                    SOL
              Nobody calls me anything.

                    DIXIE
              Not even your mother?

                    SOL
              I never had a mother. They
              found me in a garbage pail.

23  INT - HOTEL CORRIDOR - NIGHT:   DIXIE AND SOL CORRIDOR

   Sol and Dixie show cornet case and gun.  Dixie starts to
   enter, Sol says to wait.

                    DIXIE
              What kind of party is this?

                    SOL
              You never been to a party like
              this.

                    DIXIE
              Maybe I don't want to go.

                    SOL
              You do want to go.

   Dixie catches glimpses of things.  Door opens and Vince and
   Ed revealed.  Dixie talks to Vince.  Dutch enters.  He is
   happy to see Dixie.  Walks into room where some girls and
   entertainers are waiting.

24  INT - SUITE #1 - NIGHT:   DUTCH TELLS DIXIE ABOUT VERA

   Dixie enters, Dutch follows.  He tries out baby grand.

                    DUTCH
              Listen, I got a lot to do
              tonight and I got this girl
              comin'.  She sings, got her
              own music.  You read music?

                          DIXIE
                Read it, write it, play it,
                sleep with it.

                          DUTCH
                You play for her, don't sleep
                with her.  Keep her company for
                a while.  I got some shitty
                business to do and then we'll
                have a party.  (pause)  I like you.


24A   INT - HOTEL ELEVATOR - NIGHT:   <u>VERA ELEVATOR</u>

We go up with Vera Cicero in the elevator.  She looks about
three times more glamorous than she did the night in the
Bamville Club.


24C   INT - HOTEL SUITE #1 - NIGHT:   <u>DIXIE SEES VERA</u>

Many EXTREME CLOSE UPS of the party, just building.  Men are
looking over the women, who are beauties, with a hard edge
to their looks, mostly, though not with Vera.  The women are
mostly showgirls, chorines, some hookers, some aspiring
actresses.  This is a late evening, after the shows close.

JOE FLYNN enters with TWO BODYGUARDS, shakes hands with
Madden and Frenchy.  Vera goes to piano where Dixie and
Dutch are talking.

                          DUTCH
                    (to Vera)
                Hiya baby.  I got you an accomp...
                accompan... a piano player.

                          DIXIE
                The little girl.

                          VERA
                The altar boy.

                          DUTCH
                    (to Madden)
                Let's get at it.

                          MADDEN
                    (supremely calm)
                Fine.  We're set up down the
                hall.

Madden leads the way.

                    DIXIE
                (to Dutch)
          What's going on?

                    DUTCH
          Just a business deal.

Dixie tries to figure it out.

26   INT - HOTEL SUITE #2 - NIGHT:     PEACE CONFERENCE BEGINS

A table is arranged for four people: Dutch, Flynn, Big
Frenchy and Madden take seats. Vince, Abbadabba, Weinstein,
and Flynn bodyguards stand in the hallway outside door,
eyeing one another. None have pistols, all confiscated as
they came off elevator.

                    MADDEN
          I used to do this in Sing Sing.
          Cons stabbin' one another.
          Crazy. I'd tell 'em, listen,
          you'll die before you get a
          chance to serve your sentence.
          What's the point?

                    DUTCH
          ...One of his fuckin' guys
          threw a bomb at me. I don't
          know why I'm not dead.

                    FLYNN
          He hung my brother by the
          thumbs. He's a goddam
          sadist. Bughouse bastard.

27   INT - HOTEL SUITE #1 - NIGHT:     YOU SURE ARE LOW-DOWN

Dixie is at piano. Vera is seated on a chair behind him.

                    VERA
          You were very gallant sitting
          up all night with a frightened
          little girl.

                    DIXIE
          Maybe some night you'll sit
          up with me. Or assume some
          other position.

                    VERA
          That would be cheating on
          Dutch, as I understand it.

-22-

>                    DIXIE
>           Very likely.
>
>                    VERA
>           Do you like to cheat?
>
>                    DIXIE
>           No.  But in certain situations
>           I might make an exception.

Vera sits down next to him.

>                    VERA
>               (letting him play a
>                few more bars)
>           You sure are low-down.

Dixie gives her a very long look.

27A  INT - BATHROOM OF SUITE - NIGHT:  <u>KISS IN BATHROOM</u>

Vera combs her hair, finishes, opens door.  Dixie is there.
He kisses her, leaves before she can speak.

28   INT - SUITE #2 - NIGHT:  <u>PEACE CONFERENCE CONCLUDES</u>

>                    MADDEN
>           Here it ends.  You're here
>           because you both agreed to this
>           truce.  And it is a truce.
>           Tomorrow is a business day.
>           Clear?

Neither Flynn nor Dutch speak or move.

>                    MADDEN
>           Is it clear?

He looks at Flynn, who nods, then at Dutch, who barely nods.

>                    MADDEN
>           All right.  Shake hands.

Dutch and Flynn shakes hands.  All stand up.

>                    MADDEN
>           In the next room, gentlemen, is
>           the most delectable  food, drink,
>           and pussy available at any price
>           in New York.  Take a sample of
>                         (MORE)

MADDEN contd.
each and try to remember that
this is why we are working -- to
live the way kings and princes
live in this world.

30  INT - SUITE #1 - NIGHT:  <u>VERA SINGS, DIXIE PLAYS</u>

Dixie and Vera are dancing to a slow fox trot on the radio.
People are more paired off than when we last saw them.
Dixie's becoming infatuated with her.

                    DIXIE
          ...What about you?

                    VERA
          I sing and tell jokes.

                    DIXIE
          Let's hear one.

                    VERA
          Hello, sucker.

No laugh. Dixie gives her a very long look, as Dutch enters
with entourage, goes to the bar and gets himself a drink.
The Flynns hang back until Dutch clears away from the bar.
Dixie and Vera stop dancing and join Dutch.

                    DIXIE
          Is there peace in the world?

                    DUTCH
          I shook his hand. I shoulda
          cut it off.

                    DIXIE
          Cool down. You'll overheat
          and ruin your new shirt.

                    DUTCH
          You two gettin' along?

                    VERA
          We're making contact.

                    DUTCH
          You look like a beautiful
          doll. (turns to Dixie)
          You know that tune? Play
          it for me.

Dixie looks at Dutch.

                    DUTCH
          Go ahead Dixie, play it.

                    DIXIE
          Sure.

Dixie goes back to piano, plays "Oh You Beautiful Doll."
Dutch takes Vera's arm, dances. He's upset, grits teeth.

                    VERA
          Don't think about Flynn.
          Think of something pleasant,
          like my career. Can you
          really help the way you said?

                    DUTCH
          I can get anything I want in
          this town. That's why I gotta
          work so goddamn hard, payin'
          off the politicians.

                    VERA
          Politicians don't run nightclubs.

                    DUTCH
          You got a lot to learn, kiddo.

The song ends, they walk to the piano, and Dutch now has his
arm around Vera's waist, taking possession.

                    DUTCH
          Play for her, Dixie. She sings
          great.

                    DIXIE
            (to Vera)
          Okay, baby, whataya got?

                    VERA
          You know "Between the Devil and
          the Deep Blue Sea?"

Dixie swings into it and Vera sings. Dutch is ecstatic,
falling in love; a swift obsession. Dixie sees this also.

CLOSE SHOTS of gangsters and women. VIEW ON JOE FLYNN
watching also from across the room, noting Dutch's behavior.
Madden and Frenchy are less anxious about the night.
The song ends. Frenchy turns on the radio. He looks at his
watch and we HEAR Ted Husing announce he's broadcasting from
the Cotton Club. Ellington plays a tune.

                    MADDEN
          Food is ready, folks, help yourself
          in the suite across the hall.

31   INT - HOTEL SUITE #3 - NIGHT:   <u>JOE FLYNN MURDER</u>

A vast spread of food, salads, cakes, pies, huge chunk of
beef.  Behind table BLACK MEN are serving.  Mobsters move
inside, Dixie and Vera are stopped by guard.

                    MONK
          Mr. Madden first.

                    MADDEN
          Let the two kids in.

                    FRENCHY
          So all right.  We're gonna
          have a little peace and quiet
          in Harlem.  Owney did all right
          bringing you guys together.

Dutch turns to Frenchy, plate in hand.

                    DUTCH
          Get it right.  We ain't together.
          We got some territory settled,
          is what we did.  We ain't together.

                    FRENCHY
          All right, Dutch.  We know what
          we got.  But Owney is a goddamn
          diplomat, is what I think,
          putting this together.  Goddamn
          Owney oughta be in Washington,
          we wouldn't have all that shit
          goin' on in Europe.

                    FLYNN
          What I like is we keep the fuckin'
          Jews where they belong.  Keep the
          Jews and the niggers where they
          belong and we're all right.  Jews
          are nothing but niggers turned
          inside out, anyway.

VIEW ON DUTCH

He puts plate down, reaches across buffet table, grabs
carving knife from servant's hand, and in swift turn shoves
Frenchy aside, plunges knife into Flynn's chest.  He pulls
it out, plunges it in again, then again.  Blood spurts out
of Flynn's throat.  Dutch is maniacal.

VIEW ON THE CHANDELIER

Blood hits the crystals.

The whole thing happens too fast for anybody to have stopped it.  Electric behavior.  Dutch stands up from the murder, looks at Flynn, dying.

He stabs him again, stands up, then stabs again, and yet again.  This time Frenchy puts pistol to Dutch's head.

              FRENCHY
     That's enough, Dutch.

              DUTCH
     Yeah.  That's enough.

All are stunned into disbelieving silence by the suddenness and horrendousness of what they have just witnessed.  A silence, then Dutch puts the knife back on the table.

VIEW ON MADDEN

He looks at Flynn, dead, looks at Dutch, looks at Frenchy and gestures with his head to one side.  Frenchy clears room of all except Dutch, Dixie and Vera.

              MADDEN
     Somebody ought to cut out
     your brain and pickle it.
     You're the craziest son of
     a bitch I ever knew.

              DUTCH
     I-I-I get excited.  He knows
     I'm Jewish.

On Frenchy's signal, two men come and lay bedspread on the floor, roll Flynn into it and carry him off.  Dixie and Vera have not moved.  Dutch is still by the table.

              DUTCH
     Blood on your rug.

              MADDEN
     You got it on your brain.

              DUTCH
     Owney, I'm sorry.

              MADDEN
     You're bloody fuckin' sorry
     as a human being, Dutch.
     Bloody fuckin' sorry.

                    DUTCH
          I can make it all right with
          the blood.

Dutch walks to doorway, sees black bellboy.  Dutch grabs his
arm, walks him to where Flynn's blood has stained rug.
Dutch reaches in pocket, hands man a hundred dollar bill.
Frenchy follows Dutch's moves with pointed pistol.

                    DUTCH
          Nothing against you, buddy.

He then punches the black man full on the nose, knocking him
down.  He lifts him by the collar, face on the floor, and
lets his nose bleed on the rug.

                    DUTCH
          Get him to a doctor.  He's
          probably got a broken nose.

Madden is watching like the old man of the mountains.

VIEW ON VERA

A drop of blood hits her cheek.

VIEW ON DIXIE

He notices, moves his hand to wipe it wway.

CLOSE ON DIXIE'S HAND

Another drop of blood marks his hand.

VIEW -- The bloody chandelier.  Dutch turns around and looks
at Dixie and Vera.

                                        DISSOLVE:

31A  EXT - DUTCH'S DUSENBERG - NIGHT:  <u>DRIVING FAST AFTER MURDER</u>

     Driving fast down the empty streets.

32   INT - DUTCH'S CAR - NIGHT:  <u>DRIVE HOME AFTER MURDER</u>

     Dixie driving, Vera in the front seat.  Butch in back,
     fidgets with pistol.  All are trembling.

                    DIXIE
          I'll take her home.

                    DUTCH
          You're a smart guy.  She's
          smart too.  You're smart.

Dutch nervously takes pistol from shoulder holster, holds it
in his hand throughout the rest of scene.

                    DUTCH
          You two.  Jesus Christ
          I'm sorry about that.

The gun is mesmerizing Dixie.

                    DIXIE
          Listen.  Flynn almost killed
          the two of us that night too.

                    DUTCH
               (cheering up)
          That's right.  The bastard
          bombed the three of us.

He straightens visibly, thinking it out.

TWO SHOT -- Vera and Dixie reflection.

                    DUTCH
          You'd never tell what you saw.

                    DIXIE
          You don't need even to think
          about that.

                    DUTCH
          Don't get lost, either.  I
          wanna know where you are.
               (to Vera)
          Hey, kid, sit up.  Don't worry
          about it.  I got the fix in.

                    VERA
          Whatever you say, Dutch.

Dutch looks at pistol, then at Dixie, puts it away.

33   EXT - HOUSE - NIGHT:   DUTCH BACKING INTO SHADOWS

DIXIE'S POV:

Dutch is slinking through the shadowy walkway, walking
backward, looking at Dixie and Vera.

                          DUTCH
                     (barely hear him)
                ...no friends, nothing.  The
                way the cards fall.


34   INT - CAR - NIGHT:   DIXIE & VERA DISCUSS MURDER

     Dixie, Vera in front seat.  Dixie yells, gives off steam.

                          VERA
                     I need something to eat.

                          DIXIE
                     You want to eat?  You got no
                     feelings for Mr. Flynn?

                          VERA
                     He was a bootlegger.  That's how
                     they live.  Maybe one day you'll
                     wise up, sap.

     Dixie drives off.


36   INT - CAR EXT VERA'S APARTMENT - NIGHT:   DROP OFF VERA

     Dixie stops in front of house.

                          VERA
                     You didn't get my anything
                     to eat.

                          DIXIE
                     You can chew your fingernails.

                          VERA
                     Why not come in?

                          DIXIE
                     Not this time.  You don't
                     belong to me.

     She exits to house, Dixie slumps on wheel.


38   EXT - BACK ENTRANCE - NIGHT:   ENTERTAINERS ENTER

     Entertainers and musicians enter, some hanging around,
     smoking.  The Williams brothers arrive.  JOE, the man at the
     stage door greets them.  They walk up the metal stairs.

37   EXT - COTTON CLUB - NIGHT:   PATRONS ENTER

Cars arrive; excitement builds. The sophisticated white PATRONS stroll by Holmes and enter the Cotton Club. Many shots of high-class white patrons. Adults, children gawk.

39   INT - BACKSTAGE - NIGHT:   BACKSTAGE PREPARATIONS

MOVING POV:

The cubicles, the showgirls getting ready, the famous entertainers, musicians, etc., backstage life. The entertainers are all black. DUKE ELLINGTON discusses something with Herman Stark, the manager. Elida Webb is talking to the girls.

43   INT - COTTON CLUB KITCHEN - NIGHT:   KITCHEN PREPARATIONS

Food being prepared. "Porter-style" WAITERS are polite and deliberate. Chef is Chinese named LING. HEAD BUSBOY takes bets on the side, wads of cash between fingers.

43A  INT - COTTON CLUB STAIRS - NIGHT:   PATRONS UP STAIRS

High society whites moving up the carpeted stairs.

40   EXT - COTTON CLUB - NIGHT:   DWYERS ARRIVE COTTON CLUB

MOVING VIEW

Here come the Dwyers, rushing, late, in their Saturday night best. Dixie, Vince, Tish and Patsy, walking. They greet and pass Holmes with a nod, though Vince is suspicious of all blacks in positions of authority.

CLOSE ON DIXIE

Happy to take mother to hear Ellington, but still preoccupied with nightmarish events of last week.

41   INT - COTTON CLUB STAIRS - NIGHT:   DWYERS GO UP STAIRS

Dwyers go up stairs, rubbernecking like tourists. Dixie dances up the last few steps with Tish.

44  INT - COTTON CLUB - NIGHT

Fanfare o.s. "East St. Louis Toodle-oo".

At top of stairs Dixie and family meet Kid Griffin and are introduced to spectacle of Club's big opening number.

VIEW ON DIXIE

Really impressed with the club's sophistication.

45  VIEW ON THE REVUE

The "High Yaller" girls.

46  VIEW ON DWYERS IN CLUB AISLE

Stark is talking with Kid Griffin, who is in process of seating Dwyers at worst worst table in the house because of Vince's surly attitude. Griffin is obviously exasperated.

                    VINCE
          This is the best table in
          the house?

                    GRIFFIN
          The best we can do for you,
          my friend.

                    VINCE
          We're in a corner. You ain't
          no friend of mine.

Griffin smiles.

                    TISH
                (to herself)
          That's him, that's Owney.

                    DIXIE
          Who?

                    TISH
          Over there. Owney Madden.
          Now he knows about music and
          acting too. He backed Mae
          West's show last year, and
          now they call him Mr. Broadway.

Tish walks toward Madden's table. Dixie follows.

                    MADDEN
          Well, well.  A pleasure
          to see you again.

He nods at Dixie.  Dixie nods, says nothing.

                    TISH
          You know one another?

                    MADDEN
          We've met.

                    TISH
          Isn't that nice.  This is
          my son Michael, Owen.  He plays
          cornet and he's marvelous and
          he's going to be a great actor.
          You must hire him for something.

                    DIXIE
          My mother, she loves me.

                    MADDEN
          Don't you already have a job?

                    DIXIE
          I play piano here and there.
          Nothin' steady.

                    MADDEN
          You've got to be careful who
          you play piano for.  Come
          around and see me.

47    VIEW ON THE REVUE

      Girls out, Berry Brothers on.

42    INT - BACKSTAGE - NIGHT

      The Williams Brothers coming down the stairs.

                    SANDMAN
          Are you ready for you debut,
          brother?

                    CLAY
          Ready... aim... fire...

He does a wild bit of tap.

42A VIEW ON THE REVUE

"Berry Brothers", "Peters Sisters", "Rhythm Queens" in rapid succession. The sophisticated audience.

47B VIEW IN MEN'S ROOM

Madden and Frenchy together.

    MADDEN
What do you think of this
Dwyer kid?

    FRENCHY
Not impressed.

    MADDEN
I was thinking of the coast.
The kid looks good, talks
pretty.

    FRENCHY
I don't trust no one with
a nickname.

    MADDEN
What about your nickname,
Frenchy?

    FRENCHY
That's different.

    MADDEN
Why?

    FRENCHY
I'm trustworthy.

MEDIUM SHOTS

The two at the urinals.

    MADDEN
Oh, yeah. What would I
do without ya?

    FRENCHY
Right. (points to Madden's
fly)

A62  INT - BACKSTAGE - NIGHT

Sandman and Clay are wandering around backstage.  They look out towards the show, both are enchanted.

48  VIEW ON STAGE

"Shake That Thing".  During number, Vince causes disturbance.

63  INT - BACKSTAGE - NIGHT

CLOSE ON SANDMAN

Watching the show from backstage.

Lila Rose is on stage performing "Creole Love Call".

64  SANDMAN'S POV:

Lila Rose in "Creole Love Call".

48A  INT - COTTON CLUB - NIGHT

"Creole Love Song" ends and the showgirls come on and start "Bandanna Babies".  Dutch Schultz and party come up.  This includes FRANCES FLEGENHEIMER and Sol Weinstein.

                        FRANCES
      Nice place.  How come you
      never took me here before?

                        DUTCH
      I almost never come here.

                        KID GRIFFIN
      Good evening, Mr. Schultz.
      Nice to see you again.

                        FRANCES
      Do you ever tell the rruth
      to anybody?

They move through the club to a table.

49   INT - COTTON CLUB - NIGHT

VIEW ON FRENCHY

Sitting in a corner booth of the club, the management's special corner. He sees Dutch arrive.

51   INT - COTTON CLUB - NIGHT

Kid Griffin seats Dutch, Frances. Vera and Abbadabba sit at next table. Abbadabba tries, fails to amuse Vera.

                    ABBADABBA
          Ask me the square root of four
          thousand, two hundred and eighty
          eight. Ask me anything, I'm a
          genius.

                    VERA
          All right. Why didn't your
          mother raise ducks instead
          of kids?

Sol Weinstein sits to Dutch's right, Frances on Dutch's left, Vera across from Dutch, who has difficulty keeping his eyes off her. Frances notices this. Sol is with, but not of this party, merely a presence, very aloof.

                    ABBADABBA
          Mathematics is just like love.

                    VERA
          Oh yeah? Well I think your
          number's up.

VIEW ON DUTCH'S TABLE -- A waiter brings champagne.

                    DUTCH
          How 'bout that Owney, huh?
          You gonna pop the cork?

                    WAITER
          I certainly am.

                    DUTCH
          Fifty bucks if you hit the
          ceiling, huh?

50   INT - MADDEN'S OFFICE - NIGHT

Frenchy opens office door.

                    FRENCHY
          Owen, the Dutchman just
          come in.

                    MADDEN
          I don't want to talk to him
          in the club.  Up by the coop.

                    FRENCHY
          I'll tell him.

51   VIEW ON DUTCH'S TABLE

     Frenchy comes over.

                    FRENCHY
          Anything you need, Dutch?

                    DUTCH
          Bring me the moon, Frenchy.

                    FRENCHY
          It's up on the roof.  When you
          get a minute, Owen wants to
          show you his pigeons up there.

                    DUTCH
          Owney and his pigeons.  Frances,
          I'll be right back.

                    FRANCES
          Could you leave somebody with me?

     Dutch gestures to Sol, who comes over and sits down.

                    SOL
          Now you're gonna have a
          good time, so just relax.

53   VIEW ON MADDEN AND FRENCHY

                    FRENCHY
          Look at that face, Owen.

THEIR POV:

Sol Weinstein, watching the show.

                    MADDEN
          Death Yiddish style.

53A VIEW ON STAIRS

Dutch follows Frenchy up the stairs.

      DUTCH
  What is this with pet pigeons?
  I used to catch 'em and cook 'em.

      FRENCHY
  Don't tell that to Owen.

50A INT - COTTON GLUB - NIGHT

GLORIA SWANSON and her ESCORT are with Kid Griffin. Eyes of everyone in the club are on them. One Man Dance is on.

      KID GRIFFIN
  Nice to see you. I'm a fan
  of yours, Miss Swanson.

      SWANSON
   (deep, affected voice)
  How nice.

Griffin gives them a ringside table.

58 EXT - COTTON CLUB ROOM - NIGHT

Frenchy leads Dutch to the pigeon coop.

      MADDEN
  You embarrassed me very badly
  last week. (pause)
  And restitution must be made.
  It's a law of the church, it's
  a law of the land, and it's my
  law. I want $25,000 in cash,
  now. It's a bargain -- I know
  you love a bargain.

      DUTCH
   (after pause)
  That's fair. I owe you.

Dutch counts out money.

      MADDEN
  Sometimes you're a big man, Dutch.

                    DUTCH
          You know how I got that big?
          I ate a pigeon every day
          when I was a kid.

   He looks at Madden, exits.


58A  VIEW ON REVUE

   Butterbeans & Suzy do "Go Back Where You Stayed Last Night."


61  INT - BACKSTAGE - NIGHT

   A stream of CHORINES comes down from dressing rooms.
   Sandman singles out Lila Rose and follows her descent.  He
   emerges from invisibility, she sees him, he stops.

                    SANDMAN
          Be careful what you do
          to my heart.

                    LILA ROSE
          You're in love, are you?

                    SANDMAN
          I haven't been able to eat
          or sleep since late this
          afternoon.

                    LILA ROSE
          Too fast, you shouldn't fall
          so easy.

                    SANDMAN
          All I want to do is marry
          you and take you away from
          all this.

                    LILA ROSE
          Are you crazy?  I practically
          just got here.

                    SANDMAN
          Well, me too.  Let's never be
          separated.

                    LILA ROSE
          Uh, can I do this number?

   Lila Rose makes her entrance for "Creole Rhapsody".

A59  INT - COTTON CLUB - NIGHT

    VIEW ON REVUE

    "Creole Rhapsody".  CLOSE SHOTS on the Cotton Club beauties.

59  VIEW ON DIXIE

    He comes out of men's room, walks toward his table and catches the eye of Vera, on her way to ladies' room. They meet in the aisle.  The VIEW MOVES CLOSE and we can HEAR.  They look nonchalant but are not.

> DIXIE
> What are you doing here?

> VERA
> He likes to look at me.
> If his wife leaves early he
> wants me to meet him.

VIEW ON FRANCES FLEGENHEIMER

Watching impatiently for Dutch to come back.

> VERA
> He saw you were here.  He
> wants to talk to you.

> DIXIE
> I'm with my family.  I don't
> need that stuff tonight.

> VERA
> Do yourself a major favor and
> don't rile him.  You remember
> how he gets when he's riled?
>    (pause)
> Oh Christ, here he comes.

VIEW ON DUTCH

Coming at them, from the roof.

TWO SHOT -- Vera and Dixie.  They go in opposite directions. Dixie passes Dutch's table, puts his arm around drunk wandering in aisle to get past Dutch without being noticed.

54  VIEW ON THE REVUE

    Williams Brothers first spot.

56  VIEW ON THE REVUE

"The Mooche". Intercut with principals in romance and intrigue.

57  VIEW ON CLUB

The show is over. Cast is excited after finale. The orchestra plays music for dancing. Dixie takes Tish on the floor.

CLOSE ON DIXIE AND TISH

Dancing in a crowd.

VIEW ON VINCENT AND PATSY

They are dancing, trying to find orifices.

Dutch grabs Frances, goes to dance floor, dances his way across to get to Dixie and Tish.

                    FRANCES
          What the hell are you doin'?

                    DUTCH
          Will you quit bellyachin', for
          chrissake.

                    FRANCES
          What about that Vera?

                    DUTCH
          What about her?

                    FRANCES
          What's she to you?

                    DUTCH
          She's Abbadabba's girlfriend.

                    FRANCES
          She is like hell. She
          can't stand him.

                    DUTCH
          That's their problem. I
          don't worry about that.

                    FRANCES
          I thought maybe you did
          worry about it. I thought
          maybe she was your problem.

DUTCH
Listen, goddamnit. Either
behave yourself, or I'll
send you home. You hear it?

Dutch pulls, pushes Frances through crowd to Dixie and Tish.

FRANCES
Arthur, for god's sake. Are
you dancin' with me or them?

Dutch reaches them; two couples dance and talk.

DUTCH
Hey, how you doin', lucky boy?

DIXIE
People gotta be lucky when
they hang out with you,
Dutch. Meet my mother,
Tish Dwyer, one of the great
white mothers in this world.

DUTCH
And this is my wife Frances,
who likes to nag me.

TISH
How do you do? I heard
you were bombed recently.
Does that happen often?

DUTCH
It's pickin' up.

Tish laughs at this. Vince is causing scene with Patsy.
Dutch grabs Dixie's arm.

DUTCH
I wanna talk to you, Dixie.
I need a guy with your talent.

DIXIE
Musical talent?

DUTCH
Yeah, that too. But I want
you to help me get a new look.

Dixie wants to laugh, Tish is giggly.

DUTCH
Frances says I'm a slob.

                    FRANCES
          Who's got to say anything?
          Just look at you.

                    DIXIE
          Get yourself a tailor, Dutch.
          I'm a musician.

                    DUTCH
          I know you are.  I'll
          give you two hundred a week.

                    DIXIE
          Let's talk after this dance.

60  EXT - COTTON CLUB - NIGHT:  <u>DUTCH OFFERS DIXIE JOB</u>

    Dutch and Dixie come down club stairs together.

    CLOSE ON DIXIE -- Turns and looks up.

    HIS POV:

    Sol Weinstein, watching them go.

    They stop on sidewalk.  A beer truck passes by.  Dutch
    inhales; he is menacing.

                    DUTCH
          I'm gonna give you three
          hundred a week.

                    DIXIE
          You said two hundred.

                    DUTCH
          I could say fifty and you'd
          take it because I want you
          to take it.

                    DIXIE
          Guns, bombs, knives.  That's
          not my life, Dutch.  I play
          music.

                    DUTCH
              (softly, venomously)
          I'm telling you you got a job.
          All I want is for you to work
          my nightclubs, talk to the
          musicians, keep 'em happy.
                    (MORE)

                    DUTCH cont.
          And I want you to show Vera a
          good time.  She can't stand
          Abbadabba but she likes you.
               (pause)  I like you too.
               (pause)  If I didn't like you
          you'd be dead.  You understand?

                    DIXIE
          I understand.  It's nice
          to be liked.

They go back into the club, past Holmes.

                    HOLMES
          Evenin', gentlemen.
               (whispers to Dixie)
          How come you're hustlin' for
          the 'fays?

52   INT - BACKSTAGE - NIGHT

Sandman confronts Lila Rose as she comes offstage.  There is
tremendous electricity between them.

                    SANDMAN
          I gotta see you.  After the show.

                    LILA ROSE
          No.

                    SANDMAN
          Tomorrow, then.  You've gotta.

                    LILA ROSE
          At the Mighty Abyssinian
          Church at ten.

They can't help themselves; they kiss.  Lila Rose's eyes
widen as she sees someone behind Sandman.  Mike Best, huge
and hamfisted, puts a hand on Sandman's shoulder, almost
crushes it.  He gestures "cut it out."

                    SANDMAN
               (angry)
          Hey, I'm just a dancer tryin'
          to get ahead.

Best shoves him aside.

                    BEST
          Watch your act around here,
          nigger.

-43-

66  INT - COTTON CLUB - NIGHT

   VIEW ON THE AISLE -- As Dwyers leave, Dixie bumps into
   Gloria Swanson.  They manuever, apologize; she looks at him,
   he at her:  zonk.

                    SWANSON
           You're a very beautiful person.

                    DIXIE
           You're more beautiful than
           I am.

                    SWANSON
           You should be in pictures.
           You have a chance when you
           are gorgeous.

                    DIXIE
           I can't miss.

                    SWANSON
           I think not.  Come by the
           studio to see me.

   Dixie passes Vera.  They look at one another.

67  INT - BACKSTAGE - NIGHT

   Sandman is trying to talk to Lila Rose.  She's all business.

                    LILA ROSE
           I told you I can't go anywhere
           tonight.  Nowhere.

                    SANDMAN
           I don't take no for an answer.

                    LILA ROSE
           You better believe me and
           right now you better leave
           me a-lone.

   She strides out, past bubbling entertainers.  He watches.

67A EXT - ALLEY - NIGHT:   ENTERTAINERS LEAVING

   The entertainers leaving.

-44-

67B EXT - COTTON CLUB - NIGHT: <u>PATRONS LEAVING</u>

Patrons leave in taxis, cars. As excitement dies, we MOVE CLOSER to little KID, tap dancing for pennies.

DISSOLVE:

69 INT - CHURCH STAGE - DAY: <u>COMMUNITY REHEARSAL</u>

Sandman enters for his appointment with Lila Rose, who, along with other Cotton Club performers, is there teaching five dancing CHILDREN and helping the church put on a community show. Madame St. Clair is one of the organizers, along with seven other black SOCIETY LADIES. After the rehearsal, Sandman rushes to Lila Rose.

SANDMAN
You still mad at me?

LILA ROSE
I was never mad. I just felt you should respect my private life. (pause) When you stopped me on the street, didn't I say this man is gonna take a piece of my life?

SANDMAN
That's 'cause you knew it too. Let's get married now instead of havin' lunch.

LILA ROSE
Married? No chance. I'm goin' up in this world. I want <u>real</u> parts, Broadway.

SANDMAN
That's white show business.

LILA ROSE
Isn't that what it is?

SANDMAN
(ad lib)
Is there a piano player here?

He sings "Tall, Tan and Terrific." He ends, they embrace.

SANDMAN
C'mon. I gotta show you off.

They exit.

71  INT - HOOFERS CLUB - DAY:  <u>HOOFERS CLUB</u>

They enter into this social club, tables with men playing cards.  Radio is playing jazz music.  SUGAR COATES is playing blackjack with ANOTHER HOOFER.  Sandman, holding Lila Rose by the hand, goes to Sugar.

                    SANDMAN
          Sugar, I want you to marry me.

                    SUGAR
          I'm already married.

                    SANDMAN
          You're the president of this
          club.  You're just like a ship's
          captain, you can perform the
          ceremony.  And I need it now,
          Sugar.  Can't wait no longer.

                    SUGAR
               (to Lila Rose)
          You take this man to be
          your lawful wedded husband,
          you a whole lot crazier than
          he is.  (pause)  And furthermore,
          ain't no women allowed in here.

                    LILA ROSE
               (indignant)
          Why not no women?

                    SUGAR
          Because this is the <u>Hoofers</u>
          club.  The Hoofers Club.
          Lemme show you what I mean...

Sugar rises, moves to middle of floor, starts to tap dance.  Sandman crosses, Lila Rose and others start to form circle.  Each man dances 8 bars in center of circle, then eases back to let next man have his turn.

                                        DISSOLVE:

72  INT - HOOFERS CLUB - DAY:  <u>SUGAR REMINDS SANDMAN HE'S LATE</u>

The MUSIC is subdued, nobody dancing.  People again at the things they were doing before Sandman arrived.  He is at a table with Lila Rose.  Romantic MUSIC.

                    SANDMAN
          Come with me now.  I'll get
          a room and you can check
          me out.

                    LILA ROSE
          No way... no way.

                    SUGAR
          Hey, Sandman, ain't you
          runnin' numbers today?

Sandman looks at the time, panics and runs out.

73  EXT - HARLEM STREET - DAY:  <u>SANDMAN RUNS DOWN STREET</u>

Sandman running. We see Winnie running behind him, trying
to catch up.

                    WINNIE
          Hey Dalbert!  Wait!  Wait!

                    SANDMAN
          I can't wait.  I'm late.

                    WINNIE
          Wait, Dalbert, you gotta,
          you gotta!

Sandman slows down and keeps running in place, marking time,
unable to contain his anxious energy. Winnie dodges cars
and crosses the street. About six feet away she stops and
goes into her dance steps, the combination we saw earlier.

                    WINNIE
               (still dancing)
          I won the contest.

                    SANDMAN
          You're a winner, kid.  I knew
          it when you were born.  Wait
          here.

He enters the building.

74  INT - BAR - DAY:  <u>SANDMAN RUNS THRU BAR</u>

A few men are standing at the bar as Sandman rushes in.

                    MAN AT BAR
          Hey Sandman, you late.

                    SANDMAN
          Your momma's late.

Sandman enters through door. Winnie coyly peeks in.

75  INT - NUMBERS BANK - DAY:   SANDMAN LATE WITH NUMBERS

Large room full of tables and desks, fifteen people working on columns of numbers, counting money, talking on phones. Bumpy Rhodes is beside desk of Madame St. Clair.

Sandman delivers his book to man at desk next to Madame St. Clair. He looks it over, checks numbers rapidly.

> MAN
> He's got these startin' with five.

Tension with Sandman.

> SANDMAN
> You got the first number already?

> BUMPY
> Five.

> SANDMAN
> Oh shit.

> BUMPY
> Thanksgiving season, man. Everybody's heavy on 5-2-7. And you got two of 'em giving us ten dollar bets. You know we gotta lay off that kind of money and you go on dancin' someplace. What ails you, Sandman? You got a banana brain?

> SANDMAN
> (clearing throat)
> No way out?

Madame St. Clair speaks in precise language.

> MADAME ST. CLAIR
> No need to do anything now, Sandman. We can't lay this off now. You know that. We can't do anything but eat it. (pause) We will be in touch with you when the number comes in and we will let you know what the mortgage is. You dig, Sandman?

Sandman nods, exits.

76   EXT - STREET - DAY:   <u>WINNIE SAYS BUMPY LIKES HER</u>

Sandman walking abjectly, Winnie following. They cross Vince and his gang, up to no good.

> **WINNIE**
> They're mad because you were late. I know all about it. Everybody's nervous about white hoodlums comin' in. Bumpy said so.

> **SANDMAN**
> You keep that quiet, hear?

> **WINNIE**
> Did Bumpy yell at you?

> **SANDMAN**
> None of your business.

> **WINNIE**
> I'm in love with Bumpy.

> **SANDMAN**
> You stay away from gangsters or you gonna wind up in trouble.

Sugar runs up behind them.

> **SUGAR**
> Six, Sandman. Six. The last number was six. Five-two-six.

Sandman is relieved.

76A  INT - CHOP HOUSE - DAY:   <u>ABBA EXPLAINS NUMBER/DIXIE SERVITUDE</u>

Present are Vera, Dutch, Dixie, Frances, Sol and Abbadabba. Dixie is the beard for Vera. Piano player is playing pop and jazz tunes, 1920's cocktail music.

> **DUTCH**
> The trouble with this goddamn nigger numbers racket is the risk. I like things you can fix, like a horse race or a politician.

> **ABBADABBA**
> You know I think I can fix the number, Arthur.

                    DUTCH
              (doesn't believe it)
         Are you kiddin' me? What've
         you been drinkin'?

Dutch turns to Dixie.

                    DUTCH
         Hey Dixie, butt me.

Dixie fishes for a cigarette, lights it, hands it to Dutch.
Dutch doesn't acknowledge the gift, just takes it.

                    DUTCH
         Play that Beiderbecke tune,
         Dixie. You know the one I
         like. See if the piano guy
         knows it.

                    DIXIE
         I know the one.

He picks horn case off floor, takes out cornet.

                    VERA
         You take that everyplace?

                    DIXIE
              (with an edge)
         Dutch likes horn music.

                    VERA
              (sotto voce)
         His master's voice.

                    DIXIE
         Look who's talking.

                    VERA
         I'm going to get my own
         nightclub out of it.

Dixie goes to piano man, and they play "Singin' the Blues".

                    ABBADABBA
         Okay. Where do the numbers come
         from? From the pari-mutuel
         payoffs. Okay. I go to the
         track, look at the payoff totals
         on the first six races.

Frances is looking first at Dutch, then at Abbadabba during all this. She does not understand a word Abbadabba is saying. Dutch doesn't understand Abbadabba either, and to us it is doubletalk, because he delivers monologue at such a rapid pace. Yet he's being precise.

                    ABBADABBA
          Then I study the odds on the
          favorites in the seventh race,
          and I figure out what the number
          would be if each of these horses
          won. (pause) What if I don't
          like the number they'll produce
          if they win?

                    FRANCES
          I should have been a gangster
          instead of you.

                    ABBADABBA
          I place last minute bets,
          change their payoff totals,
          and that changes the last
          number. (pause) Any number
          I want.

                    DUTCH
          You can figure all that out
          in your head?

                    ABBADABBA
             (he taps his head)
          The one and only.

Frances turns to Sol.

                    FRANCES
          They're conquering the world
          with arithmetic. (pause)
          You ever play the horses?

                    SOL
          I used to race rats when I
          was a kid.

Dixie comes back to table after applause by Dutch, Frances, others. Vera, smouldering over his last line to her, cocks her head at Dixie.

                    VERA
          The service here is terrible.
          Get me a gin, will you?

Dixie, knowing what's up, snickers, goes for the gin.

        DUTCH
       (to Abbadabba)
    If you can do this we can put
    the niggers out of business
    and take over the whole Harlem
    numbers racket.

       ABBADABBA
    I'll drink to that.

Dutch and Abbadabba drink. Dixie brings gin, spills it accidentally on purpose on Vera.

        DIXIE
   Bottoms up.

Dutch sees this. Frances notices Dutch's concern.

A76 EXT - PALACE CHOP HOUSE - DAY: <u>PICK UP LAUNDRY</u>

Dutch and company are leaving. Dutch pulls Dixie aside, and Vera hangs back. Others move on. Vera hears what is said.

        DUTCH
    I saw you spill that drink.
    You ain't clumsy. I didn't
    like it. You do anything
    like that to her again I
    mess up your face.

        DIXIE
     (nods)
    I won't spill any more drinks.

        DUTCH
    And I want you to pick up my
    laundry at the chink's. Around
    the corner from the Bamville.

Dutch looks from Dixie to Vera. He winks at Vera, walks off. Vince and his thugs arrive, obsequiously reporting to Dutch. Something's up; Dutch sends them off angrily.

76B EXT - COTTON CLUB - DAY: <u>DIXIE ENTERS COTTON CLUB</u>

Dixie, nervous, enters past Holmes hosing off the sidewalk.

76C INT - C. C. STAIRS - DAY:  DIXIE MEETS WITH MADDEN

Dixie enters, out of breath as Madden and Frenchy exit.

MADDEN
The jazz kid.

DIXIE
You said I should see you.

MADDEN
You're between a rock and a hard place.

DIXIE
Yeah, you noticed.  Got any ideas for me?

FRENCHY
Too bad you ain't colored. We'd book you here.

DIXIE
Yeah, the great tragedy of my life.

MADDEN
I heard what Gloria Swanson was sayin' about you.  A lot of my cash goes different places, if you know what I mean.  Some goes to Hollywood, into the studios, into movies.  That's the new thing and you could front for us.

DIXIE
What do you mean, front?

MADDEN
You're a man of taste.

DIXIE
What about the Dutchman?

MADDEN
I'll keep the Dutchman off your back.

They exit.

DISSOLVE:

76D EXT - COTTON CLUB - DAY:   DIXIE CLOSES LIMO DOOR

Madden and Frenchy get into limo, Dixie closes door for them.

100 EXT - STREET - NIGHT:   DIXIE BUYS APPLE

Fruit stand; Dixie walks by, buys apple.  Hood steps out of shadows.

              HOOD
Your brother wants to see you.

              DIXIE
What for?

              HOOD
He needs some money, whatever you can spare.

Lights of a parked car turn on.  It pulls forward, Dixie gets in.

102 INT - CAR - NIGHT:   DIXIE SEES VINCE WOUNDED

Vince alone in back seat, Popke driving.  Dixie gets in.

              DIXIE
Have an apple.

              VINCE
You swipe this?

              DIXIE
Yeah... You can have a hundred -- I only have fifty, sixty bucks with me -- sixty-four.

              VINCE
Here's your apple.

              DIXIE
Here's your money.  You all right?

              VINCE
What?

              DIXIE
You wanna tell me about it?

VINCE
I'm goin' to the doctor.

DIXIE
What for, you okay?

VINCE
Yeah I just got a graze.
Can't go to the hospital,
though.

DIXIE
Vincent, what the hell is this?
What is this? Where'd you get it?

VINCE
Fightin' niggers.

DIXIE
I should knock you one in
the head.

VINCE
Dixie, calm down.

DIXIE
Pull over. (takes bite of
apple) Keep it.

Dixie gets out of car.

124 INT - DRESSING ROOM - DAY: <u>SANDMAN AND CLAY BREAK UP</u>

CLAY
(to Sandman)
What's that about a solo?

SANDMAN
They asked me to do a solo.

CLAY
<u>They</u> asked <u>you</u>. <u>You</u> didn't
ask <u>them</u>.

SANDMAN
I talked to them. Yeah.
Look, it's a step up. It's
good for both of us. Don't
give me trouble, shake my hand.

                              CLAY
                Shake your hand?  I oughta spit
                in your hand.  You want a solo?
                You got one, on stage and off.


102A MONTAGE: VINCE CAREER, DIXIE SERVITUDE

    Beginning of Vince's gangster career, time passes.

    Dixie serving Dutch drink at Bamville.
    Vince, cash, tommy gun firing.
    Dixie waiting to drive Vera home after Dutch gives her
    goodnight kiss.
    Dixie carrying laundry; times passes.
    Vince's gang attacks beer joint; beer pours on floor.
    Dixie walking Frances' two dogs.
    Vince handing out cash to members of his gang.
    Dixie changing tire on Dusenberg while Vera waits
    impatiently.


136 INT - STUDIO - DAY:  SCREENTEST

    VIEW ON SILVER SCREEN

    CLOSE on a movie slate.

    We see the screentest of Dixie as "Mob Boss" and TWO STUDIO
    EXECUTIVES discussing it.

                                              DISSOLVE:

86  EXT - VERA'S APARTMENT - NIGHT:  TAXI PICKS UP VERA

    A taxi picks up Vera and drives off.


87  INT - TAXICAB - NIGHT:  DRIVE TO BAMVILLE

    Vera and Dixie sit in taxicab.

                              VERA
                Quit lookin' at me, sucker.
                Where's Dutch?

                              DIXIE
                Dutch can't make it tonight.
                I'm your escort.

                              VERA
                Where's he taking us?  We're
                not heading toward the theatre.

                    DIXIE
          We're not going to the theater.

                    VERA
          What is this?  Am I being
          kidnapped?

                    DIXIE
          Would you like that?  I'm
          probably up to it.  You do
          move me in unusual places.

                    VERA
          Where?  Your appendix?

                    DIXIE
          Just one night, you and me.
          That'd be, what we call,
          copacetic.

                    VERA
          You mean we could both float
          around Harlem lovely drunk,
          and never go to bed until it
          was tomorrow?

                    DIXIE
          Sounds good, doesn't it?  And
          I'd know just what to do with
          tomorrow in that  case.

                    VERA
          Yeah.  You look like you would.

She pushes him away.

88  INT - BAMVILLE CLUB - NIGHT:  <u>YOU LOOK TERRIBLE</u>

Dixie and Vera enter and sit at table near band.  There is
obviously tension between them as they eat.

                    DIXIE
          My favorite lady of long ago.
          Whatever happened to you?

                    VERA
          Same thing that happened to
          you only it looks like I can
          handle it better.  You look
          terrible.

                    DIXIE
          I look great.  It's what I
          look at that ain't so great.

                    VERA
          Then quit lookin', sucker.

She guzzles her booze.

89  EXT - BAMVILLE CLUB - NIGHT:   SOL LOOKS IN BAMVILLE

Sol Weinstein gets out of car, goes to club door, looks in,
sees Vera and Dixie at table.  Watches.

                                        DISSOLVE:

93  INT - BAMVILLE CLUB - NIGHT:   LOOK AT ME TONIGHT

Dixie and Vera.

                    DIXIE
          I never quite know what to make
          of you.

                    VERA
          I know all about you.  I can
          imitate your walk, and the
          way you play your cornet.
               (she imitates him)
          You have been watched.  (pause)
          A girl needs somebody in her
          imagination.

                    DIXIE
          I feel like I'm working nights
          in somebody's dream.

                    VERA
          Pretty hot dreams.

                    DIXIE
          I know some things about you too.
          How you look when you make love.

                    VERA
          When did you see that?

                    DIXIE
          Ever since that night I put
          you to bed.

Dixie notices Sol at doorway.

                DIXIE
     The Golem has arrived.

HIS POV:

Sol Weinstein entering, taking seat at end of bar, watching.

                VERA
     He follows me everywhere.

                DIXIE
     The Golem is in love.

                VERA
     Don't be ridiculous. He's
     just keeping tabs on me for
     Dutch.

Dixie's face hardens. Band plays after intermission and he turns his attention to the music, willfully rejecting Vera.

                VERA
       (testily)
     Look, I was the one that was
     kidnapped. We could've gone
     to the theater. (pause)

                DIXIE
     Why do I feel like I'm walking
     somebody's dog. Wanna dance?

Dixie gets up, walks around and practically yanks her away from the table.

                DIXIE
     Dutch likes it when we dance.

He moves her out on the floor where a few others are dancing.

                DIXIE
     I used to dance for a living.

                VERA
     No kidding.

                DIXIE
     Yeah, I danced in tea rooms
     when I was eighteen.

                    VERA
          Tell me all about it.

                    DIXIE
          Ladies paid me to put my arms
          around them and waltz them off
          their feet.  Two bucks an afternoon
          and extra money for night work,
          if I could stand it.

                    VERA
          Could you?

                    DIXIE
          Look at me tonight.

Vera slaps him; he shoves her in return.  Other dancers
think it's a new dance rage.  They dance more savagely.
This has the elements of an Apache dance, seems
choreographed.  Vera tries to bring it off, laughing,
tossing her hair.  Crowd gets the idea, clears away.

VIEW ON SOL WEINSTEIN

VIEW ON DIXIE

Twirling Vera and sending her sliding on the floor.  She
slips, falls.  Audience becomes involved, applauds.

VIEW ON VERA

Getting up, looking contemptuously at Dixie.

VIEW ON SOL

He stands up from bar, moves toward dance floor.  Vera sees
him coming, moves back to Dixie and kisses him.

VIEW ON DIXIE

He sees Sol approaching, understands what Vera's doing.

                    DIXIE
          Okay, let's quit it.  I'm
          sorry.

                    VERA
          Sure you are.

                    DIXIE
          It wasn't you, it was me.
          Let's get out of here.

-61-

They start to leave. Dixie separates from Vera and walks in range of Sol, speaks to him.

                   DIXIE
          I'll dance with you next
          time, Sol.

He takes Vera's arm and they leave.

93A EXT - STREET - NIGHT: <u>HEADLIGHTS</u>

Headlights of their taxi. SUPERIMPOSE eye in center. Eye is of Sol Weinstein, always watching them.

94 INT - DWYER APARTMENT - NIGHT: <u>DIXIE/VERA IN KITCHEN</u>

Dixie and Vera enter very quietly, Vera's dress badly ripped. She sits at kitchen table. He goes into his bedroom and finds one of Patsy's dresses, comes out with it.

                   DIXIE
          Try this on.

Vera stands up, holds dress against herself, looks right. Dixie moves into kitchen, takes down two glasses, opens refrigerator. They sit at kitchen table, and Dixie pours lemonade and raises a toast.

                   DIXIE
          To anything.

He leans forward to kiss her and almost knocks her off her chair. Noise. They have been talking in whispers.

                  TISH o.s.
         Is that you, Vincent?

                   DIXIE
         It's Michael, Ma. It's okay,
         go to sleep.

                   VERA
           (smiling)
         Michael.

The ice is really broken now. They're comfortable with one another. He leans over and kisses her.

                   VERA
         Where do I change?

                    DIXIE
                 (pointing)
             Be my guest.


95   INT - DIXIE'S BEDROOM - NIGHT:  <u>VERA UNDRESSING</u>

     Vera goes into room, Dixie follows, puts on light.  She
     turns her back to him, points to buttons on back of dress.

                    DIXIE
             I wonder if this is my real
             job in life, taking off your
             clothes.

                    VERA
             You think of a better one?

                    DIXIE
             Not at the moment.  You feel
             like you're on your honeymoon?

                    VERA
             Honeymoons are never this
             dangerous.  If he came in
             now he'd kill us right here.

                    DIXIE
             Will you forget about him?

                    VERA
             Who?

                    DIXIE
             You never stop telling jokes.

                    VERA
             I don't feel very funny.
             I feel like things are
             better than they've ever
             been for me, but all wrong.

                                          DISSOLVE:

96   INT - DWYER APARTMENT - NIGHT:  <u>DIXIE SAYS HE'S QUITTING</u>

     They are still entwined, not making love.

                    DIXIE
             ...I'm quitting the Dutchman.
             No more running after his
             cigarettes while he strokes
             you.

VERA
How can you quit?  What else will you do?

DIXIE
The movies.  Maybe it's a pipe dream, maybe it isn't.  I just know I'm getting that son of a bitch out of my life.

VERA
You're a tough guy.

DIXIE
I get tough when I think I'm in love.

VERA
You think you're in love.

DIXIE
Yeah.  What do you think?

VERA
Flies in my brain.  I can shoo them away if I want.

DIXIE
You don't have to put up with it.  Just let's go.  Right now.

VERA
How far would we get?

DIXIE
When we get to the moon we'll worry about that.

DISSOLVE:

98  INT - DWYER APT - NIGHT:  NOT REAL LIFE - IT'S JAZZ

VERA
Is the honeymoon almost over?

DIXIE
I think so.

VERA
Will we live happily ever after?

                    DIXIE
          I don't think so.

                    VERA
          No.  (pause)  That's not
          how it goes in real life.

                    DIXIE
          This isn't real life.

                    VERA
          What is it?

                    DIXIE
          Jazz.

                                        DISSOLVE:

97   INT - DWYER APT - NIGHT:  TEA & TOAST WITH PSYCHOPATH (:30)

     They are quiet, holding one another.

                    DIXIE
          ...Who does it straight in this
          world?  You want to do it
          straight, you can't even find
          any straight.  The only way is
          to go over the top, over the
          edge, around, through, anyway
          you can.  That's how I see it.
          But some things you don't do.
          You can't watch a murder and
          then come home and fuck your
          friend who loves you and then
          leave him, and go home and wake
          up in the morning and have tea
          and toast with the psychopath.
          You can't do that.  (pause)  Can
          you?

                    VERA
          Yes.

     She gets off him and walks away.

                                        DISSOLVE:

A77  INT - DUTCH'S APT. LOBBY - DAY:  DUTCH HAS NEW SUIT

     Dixie, Dutch and Frances in lobby, Frances with her poodles.
     Dutch in new suit, looks at reflection in mirror.

                    DUTCH
          What about this suit?  Do
          I look like a boss?

                    DIXIE
          Keep two thugs behind you
          and you will.

                    DUTCH
               (still looking at self)
          I don't want 'em looking at
          the bozos behind me.  I want
          'em to notice the suit.

                    FRANCES
          Spill a little gravy on it
          like you always do.  They'll
          notice it.

They walk outside.

B77 EXT - DUTCH'S APARTMENT - DAY:   DIXIE BREAKS WITH DUTCH

They come out of the building.

                    FRANCES
          You know Dixie took a screentest?

                    DUTCH
          You took a screentest?
          What's a screentest?

                    DIXIE
          They shot some film of me and
          now they want to make a movie.

                    DUTCH
          That means Hollywood?

                    DIXIE
          Yeah, I guess it does.

                    DUTCH
          Forget it.

                    FRANCES
          Whataya mean, forget it?
          It's his big chance.

                    DIXIE
          They want me to play a gangster.
          I imitated you, Dutch...
          "Get over here or you're dead...
          Do what I say or I'll drill ya."

Dutch wants to crack Dixie's head.

                    DIXIE
          Owney arranged it. He's
          partners with the money
          guys in the picture.

                    DUTCH
          Owney's got money in it?

Dutch ponders this, his eyes angrily narrow.

                    DIXIE
          He said you wouldn't mind
          if I left for the coast.

Dutch understands he must let Dixie out of his grasp, but he doesn't like it.

                                        DISSOLVE:

77  INT - COTTON CLUB - NIGHT:  STORMY WEATHER

    INSERT:  MOVE IN on the program:

    "COTTON CLUB PARADE -- 22ND EDITION -- FALL 1929

    Scene 11.  CABIN IN THE COTTON CLUB
               SONG -- STORMY WEATHER"

                                        RAIN WIPE:

VIEW ON THE STAGE

Log-cabin backdrop and a single lamppost. Lila Rose leans against lamppost, a deep-blue spotlight on her. She sings "Stormy Weather." With help of special lighting effects, female dancers are blended into tableau as storm clouds.

                                        DISSOLVE:

Storm clouds darken and break into rain.

                                        CLOUD WIPE:

## 78: DEPRESSION/NUMBERS MONTAGE (RAIN/WIND)

Electric sign races across frame: "Stocks Crash -- Wall Street Panics! November 30, 1929" Falling money, collapsing bank accounts. Stores, factories, banks close. Tickertape ribbon spills on floor; superimpose electric sign: "Stocks Crash -- Wall Street in an Uproar."

Six dancers; feet turn into breadline feet. Out of work men play checkers on fruit crates; people sleep on stoop with newspapers. Cook in window, sign reads "Peace home-cooked meals 10 to 15¢." Desperate people ask for money, women beg. People look through garbage.

Champagne corks explode; stacked champagne glasses overflow. Partygoers walk arm in arm, laughing. Martini glass with olive, red fingernails scoop caviar. Neon signs, clinking lights. Cocktail shaker, seltzer bottle squirts. Girls laugh. People dance the night away.

Roll of dice, seven comes up. Vera lives in luxury. Dixie has shoes shined on train. Dutch has picture taken from professional photographer. Frances with cheap fur piece. Dutch makes out with Vera. Vera laughs, makes fan of paper money, peeks from behind it.

Vince and gang walk with Dutch, push people aside. Vince gives Dutch money. Boys play cops and robbers; angry black woman looks out window.

Dixie films "Mob Boss." Jazz instruments, extreme angles. Steam comes out of waiter's tray in Cotton Club. Cotton Club orchestra reed section (crowded into frame) picks up phrase. Madden draws horses. Sugar coaches Sandman on solo act, dancing faster and faster. Lila Rose sips champagne with a white man.

More "Mob Boss." Lila and Sandman twirl around and around, with camera above, on an empty dark Cotton Club stage, late at night after the club has completely emptied out.

MUSIC segues to "Black and Tan Fantasy."

Tommy gun fires. Vince and Ed throw beer bottles at black banker. Vince's gang takes money from runners, roughs them up, burns banker with cigarette. Car on sidewalk runs runner down.

Gang enters shop, fires guns and exits. Car drives by, guns fire. Vince kills two men, drives away. View on gun firing out car window. Vince's car and police car drive side by side, firing. Vince's car and black bankers car side by side, firing.

The "Mob Boss" trailer. Dixie is a convincing movie gangster.

"Ill Wind" finale. It is now the '30's.

85  INT - NUMBERS BANK - DAY:  <u>JEWETT OFFERS GUNS</u>

Madame St. Clair is with several NUMBERS BANKERS, plus BUB JEWETT, who is of a different order from the bankers. He's a gangster, they are gamblers.

> MADAME ST. CLAIR
> We're here because Mr. Jewett
> says he can protect us from
> the white invader.

> JEWETT
> I know how the Dutchman thinks.
> I see him operate with the Flynns.
> You meet a gun with a gun, and I
> got all the guns anybody ever need.

He looks each of them in the eye. All looks return to Madame St. Clair.

> MADAME ST. CLAIR
> Mr. Jewett, I think we'll pass
> on your offer. We are not
> interested in going to war.

> JEWETT
> You don't know you already
> lost the war.

135A  INT - OFFICE - DAY:  <u>ABBA FIXES 527</u>

VIEW ON ABBADABBA

On telephone, going over parimutuel sheets, racing forms, mumbling what he is doing as he works.

80  CONTD:  <u>NUMBERS WAR MONTAGE</u>

JEWETT JOINS DUTCH
MADAME ST. CLAIR NEWSPAPERS

127C INT - BACKSTAGE - NIGHT:   SANDMAN/LILA AFTER SHOW

After the show; Sandman and Lila Rose backstage with exiting entertainers. Sandman is well-dressed, clearly a star now. Admirers stop to congratulate him, ask for autographs. Sandman pulls Lila Rose aside.

                    SANDMAN
        Lila, listen, you can't do
        this to me.

                    LILA ROSE
        Do what?

                    SANDMAN
        Disappear like you do.
        Where do you go all day?

                    LILA ROSE
        I live my private life.

He pulls her away from crowd; kitchen beckons.

                    SANDMAN
        C'mon. Can't talk here with
        all these people.

                    LILA ROSE
        We're not supposed to go in
        there.

But he pulls her after him.

99  INT - BAMVILLE CLUB - NIGHT:   VINCE WRECKS BAMVILLE

Club is doing light business; Madame St. Clair at end of bar. Schultz's men enter suddenly in force: Vince Dwyer, Ed Popke, Jewett. They shoot up the place.

                    VINCE o.s.
        The Dutchman thinks you should
        join him in the numbers business.

                    MADAME ST. CLAIR
        Bumpy!

Bumpy comes out of office, kills Jewett's hood. Vince and his men escape.

127D EXT - KITCHEN - NIGHT:   SANDMAN/LILA IN KITCHEN

Sandman and Lila Rose are kissing.

VIEW ON DOOR

Mike Best emerges. Lila Rose and Sandman separate, show instant fear.

> BEST
> You son of a bitch, you're more trouble than you're worth.

Best grabs Sandman and slaps him. Lila Rose screams. Best throws Sandman on chopping board and menaces him with meat cleaver.

> BEST
> You gonna behave yourself, nigger?

> SANDMAN
> Yes. Yes. I'm gonna behave.

80B NEWSPAPER MONTAGE:   527 HITS

HEADLINES COMING OFF THE PRESS:

"527 -- A Disastrous Day For Numbers Bankers"
"Harlem Numbers Racket Invaded"
"$6,000 A Day Collections Shrink to $685"

84  INT - NUMBERS BANK - DAY:   527 HITS - NUMBERS MEETING

INSERT: A hand writes 527 on blackboard. A disaster for all black bankers, who can't cover the Thanksgiving number.

> MADAME ST. CLAIR
> Five-two-seven, again. Who can cover their bets and who cannot?

> BIG JOE ISON
> I can't, Madame St. Clair. I can cover a third, but who's going to cover me?

> MADAME ST. CLAIR
> I have three, Holstein.

> HOLSTEIN
> Where are we gonna get the rest of the money?

-69-

                    MADAME ST. CLAIR
          What about you, Flores?

                    FLORES
          Madame St. Clair -- I can't help
          you. I barely have enough to
          cover my own bets.

                    MADAME ST. CLAIR
          But for sure, we cannot get it
          from the Dutchman. We have
          to help each other. We cannot
          get it from Dutchman.

127E INT - COTTON CLUB BACKSTAGE - NIGHT:  <u>LILA ROSE QUITS</u>

     Lila Rose is furiously throwing clothes into suitcase.

                    LILA ROSE
          I'm quitting. I've made my
          choice.

135 INT - BLACK SPEAKEASY - NIGHT:  <u>STAY BLACK AND DIE</u>

     Sandman, Sugar Coates and Bumpy are at a bar together.
     Blues in background.

                    SANDMAN
          What am I supposed to do,
          just take it and say nothing?

                    SUGAR
          What <u>can</u> you do about it?

                    SANDMAN
          Beat on him. Kill him.

                    BUMPY
               (laughs)
          What world are you livin' in,
          Sandman? Take on the most
          powerful white mob in the city?
          You get Madden on your ass you
          really got somebody on your ass.

                    SUGAR
          There's only one way you can get
          even with Mike Best, Sandman. Treat
          him like a fireplug, piss on him.

                    SANDMAN
          I'll piss on his grave!

                    BUMPY
          You can dance on his grave...
          I can kill him... but I'm not
          no dancer, Sandman, I'm a pimp
          and a gambler and a thief. I got
          no talent to dance myself where I
          wanna go, and I won't work Pullmans
          for nickels and I ain't goin' back
          to Africa and run around in my
          underwear. There's only two things
          I gotta do in this life: I gotta
          stay black and I gotta die. White
          people haven't left me nothin' but
          the underworld. That's where I
          dance, Sandman. Where do you dance?

                    SANDMAN
          I'm gonna kill him with my
          tap shoes.

They raise their glasses in a toast.

                    MACHINE GUN AND TAP SHOES OPTICAL:

105 EXT - VERA'S CLUB - NIGHT:  SANDMAN/LILA OUTSIDE VERA'S

Sandman waits as crowds of white clubgoers enter. Madden's
limo pulls up, and Maden and Dixie step out. Dixie's
treated almost as an equal by Madden, now that he's made it
in the movies.

                    DIXIE
          Owney, what's the point of
          seein' Dutch?

                    MADDEN
          The point is him seein' you
          with me. And that dame
          invited us.

They enter the new club. Sandman tries to get in, is
barred, though well dressed. He studies photo of Lila Rose
with a new name: "Angelina: Lovely Songbird." She comes
out.

                    LILA ROSE
          How'd you find me?

                    SANDMAN
          You may be passin' for white,
          baby, but you ain't invisible.

He gestures toward her photo as 'Angelina'.

                    SANDMAN
          What time you through?

                    LILA ROSE
          Two a.m.

                    SANDMAN
          I'll be here.

103 INT - VERA'S CLUB - NIGHT:  <u>VERA'S CLUB CELEBRATION</u>

SIX CHORUS GIRLS come on and start to kick and bounce in their scanties. Vera walks over to Dutch's table as Dixie and Madden arrive.

                    DUTCH
          What's Madden doing here?

                    VERA
          I invited him.

                    DUTCH
          Why?

                    VERA
          I always liked his bald head.

                    DUTCH
          You invite the mick? (nasty tone)
          What part of him do you like?

Madden and Dixie enter, are seated at table next to Dutch. Dutch grudgingly greets them, hovers over their table.

                    DUTCH
                (to Dixie)
          Yeah, what's this I been
          readin' about that movie
          you're doin'... mob boss
          stuff.  They say you copied
          your style from real bosses.

                    DIXIE
                (with sardonic grin)
          You taught me everything I
          know about hoodlums, Dutch.

Abbadabba has cute HARLOT on his lap and she's smothering him with affection. Vera steps onto floor.

-72-

                    VERA
               (her own style)
          Hello, chumps.  Everybody's
          here tonight, everybody who's
          somebody.  If you're not
          somebody, you're not here and
          that's all there is to it...
          There's Mr. Broadway himself,
          Mr. Owney Madden, and back from
          Hollywood, where he's just
          finished his first movie, Dixie
          Dwyer.

Tension between Dutch and all parties as she does routine.

                    VERA contd.
          ...You know, there comes a time
          in every girl's life when her
          man needs fifty bucks...  I used
          to pass out fifties like they
          were cigar wrappers...  I
          refused a guy once and he says
          to me, Vera, reach down in your
          heart and get me a little
          cracked ice...  Love...  You can
          have it...  It winds up leading
          to marriage and that's taking
          things too far...

Sol comes to Dutch.

                    SOL
               (whispers)
          Some garbage's out back, wants
          to talk to you.

                    VERA
          ...Now, introducing Angelina,
          the lovely songbird, formerly
          with Ruth Etting and her Blue
          Belles.

Lila Rose starts "Them There Eyes" as Dutch exits.  Audience accepts her as white.

103A INT - BACK VERA'S - NIGHT: <u>VINCE BREAKS WITH DUTCH</u>

Dutch and Sol see Vince and Ed Popke waiting.  While Dutch talks to Vince Sol stares through Popke.

                    DUTCH
          Whataya say, wise guy.

                    VINCE
          I wanna talk money, Dutch.
          I'm not makin' enough. I
          get shot up, nobody gives
          a shit.

                    DUTCH
          Part of the game. How much
          you need?

He pulls out roll of bills.

                    VINCE
          I'm talking real money. Me
          and him, (indicates Popke)
          we delivered half of Harlem,
          for chrissake. On your plate.
          But I'm still making peanuts.
             (pause) I want a percentage
          of the numbers take.

                    DUTCH
          Are you outa your head? You
          handle a gun and you think
          you're the boss. I'll give
          you a raise, is what I'll do.
          Hundred more a week.
               (nods at Popke)
          And he gets fifty. Is that fair?

                    VINCE
          Fair? Shove your hundred up
          your ass, Dutch.

He turns to go. We HEAR applause outside. New song starts.

                    ED
               (turning)
          Shove the fifty up Sol's ass.

Vince and Popke go out. We HEAR Vera singing the verse of "Am I Blue" with trumpet obbligatos.

104 INT - VERA'S CLUB - NIGHT: <u>DUTCH SEES DIXIE/VERA IN LOVE</u>

Dutch comes back, tries to compose himself. He finds Dixie accompanying Vera on the trumpet.

CLOSE ON DUTCH - looking.

CLOSE ON VERA - singing.

CLOSE ON DIXIE - playing for her.

MOVE IN ON DUTCH. We can see the jealousy in his eyes.

                    DUTCH
         Didn't you have a pet snake
         once?

                    SOL
         Yeah. I couldn't trust him.
         I had to cut his head off.

113 INT - HOTEL - NIGHT: <u>SANDMAN/LILA ROSE REGISTER</u> (1:00)

Sandman, Lila Rose approach the hotel register.

                    CLERK
            (sternly)
         We don't accept mixed couples.

                    SANDMAN
         Good, 'cause we're colored.

Lila Rose looks very white indeed to the clerk.

                    CLERK
            (to Lila Rose)
         What color are you?

                    LILA ROSE
         My mother was white, my father
         was colored, so what does that
         make me?

                    CLERK
            (handing key)
         Room 428.

114 INT - HOTEL ROOM - NIGHT: <u>SANDMAN/LILA LOVE SCENE</u>

Sandman, Lila Rose on bed. They kiss passionately.

                    SANDMAN
         Some music?

                    LILA ROSE
         That'd be good...

Sandman goes to radio, turns on music. He lets his pants drop, dives into bed.

SANDMAN
People really do think you're white.

LILA ROSE
I was white for six months before I met you, workin' for a lawyer. I told you I had a private life.

SANDMAN
Why'd you do that?

LILA ROSE
Becuase I can.

SANDMAN
So what?

LILA ROSE
So don't judge me. The lawyer paid me twice the money the Cotton Club paid me. And Vera pays me five times that -- she don't ask if I'm white or colored. I'm just a human being.

SANDMAN
Vera's doorman won't let me in to hear you sing. I can't pass.

LILA ROSE
Oh, Dalbert... just make love to me.

They go at it, softly, lovingly.

107A EXT - ALLEY - NIGHT:  SHAKE

Sol Weinstein stalks something. He turns, and there is Ed Popke. Sol reaches out as if he wants to shake hands.

SOL
Shake.

ED
Shake? Why do you want to talk to me?

SOL
Shake.

                    ED
          Forget it.

Ed extends his hand tentatively. A gunshot from Sol's
extended sleeve. Ed doubles over.

                    SOL
          I don't shake hands with vipers.

Sol dumps him in the garbage.

115 EXT - STREET NEAR COTTON CLUB - DAY:   <u>BURN THAT JEW</u>

Sol walks briskly along.

                    VINCE o.s.
          That yellow rat.

CLOSE ON VINCE

Watching from a distance. He turns to one of his men.

                    VINCE
          I'm gonna burn that Jew
          to hell!

116 EXT - STREET - DAY:   <u>BABY KILLING</u>

Some kids are playing; one has a lemonade stand, another is
peddling a toy. Sol walks by. Suddenly, two cars roar by,
spitting out machine gun fire. People scream and run. Sol
picks up a child to protect himself, finally drops her and
is hit, falling into garbage can.

117 INSERT:  Newspaper headline: (:10)

          "MAD DOG BABY KILLER..." etc.

Superimposed over Vince Dwyer looking in mirror.

117A INT - COTTON CLUB - NIGHT:   <u>FRENCHY GETS MESSAGE</u>

Backstage, the usual frenzy, and Big Frenchy is walking
through. He meets Joe, the back doorman.

                    JOE
          Fella outside says he's an
          old friend of yours, Frenchy.

                        FRENCHY
              Why don't he come in?

                         JOE
              You don't want him in here.

Frenchy wonders what that means, goes out back door.

117B EXT - COTTON CLUB - NIGHT:  <u>FRENCHY KIDNAPPING</u>

Frenchy sees a man huddled several feet from doorway,
dressed in rags.  He looks like a bum.

                        FRENCHY
              You wanna see me?

Vince Dwyer looks up from under a battered hat and points
pistol at Frenchy's belly.

                         VINCE
              Exactly right.

He motions Frenchy out to the street and as they near a
waiting car, its door opens.  The gun now in his rib,
French follows Vince's gestures, enters car.

117C INT - VINCE'S CAR - NIGHT:  <u>FRENCHY IN CAR</u>

Others of Vince's hoods are waiting.

                        FRENCHY
              What's this all about?  I
              thought you specialized in
              killing kids.  I'm over
              twenty-one.

                         VINCE
              We don't wanna kill you,
              Frenchy.  We like you.  We
              just need a little money.

Car is moving.

                        FRENCHY
              What kind of money you
              talking about?

                         VINCE
              Thirty-five thousand.  I
              figure Madden'll pay that
              to get you back.

FRENCHY
Are you crazy? That cheap
bastard wouldn't pay more
than $500.

VINCE
If that's the case, Frenchy,
you better think of somebody
else who likes you. Somebody
with money.

117D EXT/INT - BAMVILLE - NIGHT:  <u>VERA SEES DIXIE AT BAMVILLE</u>

Vera arrives alone in taxi, goes to club, sees Dixie playing in band. He spots her, leaves his chair and comes to door.

X117 EXT - BAMVILLE CLUB - NIGHT:  <u>VERA WARNS DIXIE</u>

Vera and Dixie together in the shadows by the door, just out of the light.

DIXIE
I'm glad to see you.

VERA
Tell me more. No, don't tell
me anything, show me.

Dixie kisses her.

VERA
Delicious, but that's not why
I came. You may be in trouble
because of your brother.

Dixie nods, solemnly.

DIXIE
No news there. The whole
family's got the jitters,
even cousins we haven't
seen in years.

VERA
I heard some talk... Dutch's
guys. "If we can't get the
mick then let's get his
brother." Like that.

DIXIE
I'm not gonna go in hiding.

                    VERA
          Do what you do, but watch out
          for dark streets. Like this
          one. Everybody knows you hang
          out here. So that's it and
          I gotta get back. He'll be
          lookin' for me.

                    DIXIE
          So you're worried about me.

                    VERA
          Not so it shows.

He kisses her.

                    DIXIE
               It shows.

As they talk a limo pulls onto street and heads toward them. They watch it come, watch it pull close to curb in perhaps a threatening way, then stop just in front of them. Rear window is rolled down and Dixie moves Vera toward an alley.

                    VOICE FROM CAR
          Hey Dixie!

Dixie backs into the shadows. Driver of car gets out, and it is Monk, Madden's man.

                    MONK
            Owney wants to talk to you,
            Dixie.

Dixie and Vera look at one another, relieved, tense, they smile, kiss.

                    VERA
            See you later, lover.

She runs down street toward where cab is waiting for her. Dixie goes to Madden's limo.

117E INT - MADDEN'S LIMO - NIGHT:   <u>MADDEN & DIXIE IN LIMO</u>

Owney Madden, dressed in black tie, sits in the back seat. Dixie, a little nervous, looks at him.

                    MADDEN
            Your brother's become a major
            pain in the ass to everybody.
            (pause) He snatched Frenchy
            two hours ago.

                    DIXIE
          Oh Jesus, that crazy son of
          a bitch.

                    MADDEN
          You didn't know about it.

                    DIXIE
          Why should I know about it?

                    MADDEN
          I'm asking you a question.

                    DIXIE
          My brother's obviously gone
          his own way.

                    MADDEN
          You're a smart man.  Your
          brother is bound for the
          graveyard.

Dixie winces, but knows it's the reality.

                    MADDEN
          He called me.  (pause)  An
          hour ago.  (pause)  He only
          trusts you to carry the money.

Madden hands Dixie an envelope.

                    MADDEN
          Fifty.  Count it.

Dixie holds envelope, looks into it, doesn't count it.

X118 INT - CHEAP HOTEL - NIGHT:   <u>VINCE LOOKS OUT WINDOW</u>

Vince is lying on the bed.

                    MADDEN o.s.
          They'll pick you up on the
          waterfront.  Nobody's gonna
          follow you.  Nobody...

He stands and comes to window to peer out, and we SEE a
reflection of Dixie playing the cornet.  As the tune ends,
Dixie's image fades away and Vince returns to the bed.

118 INT - CHEAP HOTEL - NIGHT: <u>DIXIE RANSOMS FRENCHY</u>

CLOSE ON DIXIE'S SHOES -- Going up the stairs.

      MADDEN o.s.
  ...I'm doing exactly what your
  crazy fuckin' brother told me
  to do because I want Frenchy
  back safe.

Dixie is being led up the stairs by one of Vince's hoods.
Hood knocks at a door and it opens a crack, gun barrel comes
out, points at Dixie. Dixie laughs.

      DIXIE
  Hey, I'm Vince's brother.

      HOOD
  Gee, I saw you in the picture.

Gun retreats, door opens, hood enters first, then Dixie,
then second hood. We see Vince and henchmen. The room
looks like an arsenal, with rifles, pistols, machine guns.

      DIXIE
  Christ almighty, Vincent, are
  you out to conquer the world?
  You got an arsenal here.

      VINCE
  You got the money?

      DIXIE
  What the hell happened to you?
  How did you get this wrong?

Dixie gives Vince envelope with money. Vince counts it.

      VINCE
  I wasn't in the car when those
  kids got it, Dix. Mad Dog, for
  chrissake. I mean I wanted
  that Golem in the deep six,
  but I wouldn't shoot a kid.

      DIXIE
  Somebody shot 'em. Three or
  four kids.

      VINCE
  Crazy kids. Nobody figured
  that'd happen.

DIXIE
Where's Frenchy?

VINCE
In the bedroom. He's all right. You're taking him, you know that?

DIXIE
So I'm told.
(suddenly blows)
What is this goddamn thing, Vincent? You got the whole fucking world at war. You see Winchell's column this morning? He calls you the town's Al Capone.

VINCE
Yeah. And they're bringing in Chicago shooters to get me. Good luck.
(pause, emotional)
How's Ma?

DIXIE
Ma. Ma. You know what she's going through.

VINCE
Does everybody hate me?

DIXIE
They don't know you. They hate shootin' a kid. So you say that wasn't you, yeah, but the kid's still dead and you're gonna take the rap.

They both now know conversation is at an end. A silence.

DIXIE
Where's Frenchy?

Vince motions to a hood and the hood opens bedroom door, goes in, undoes Frenchy, who is tied to a chair. Dixie goes to doorway, looks in, sees Frenchy being untied.

VINCE
Dixie had nothing to do with this, Frenchy. You see that, don't you?

                FRENCHY
    I see what I see.  I hear what
    I hear.  And then I make up my
    own mind.

                DIXIE
              (to Vince)
    You see what being a messenger
    gets me?  (more touching)
    I'll see you later, brother.
    I hope.  Try to get yourself out
    of this town.  And I mean now.

                VINCE
    I can't.  Eddie Popke's dead.
    I got a few loose ends to take
    care of.  (to Frenchy)  Tell
    him we didn't hurt you, Frenchy.

He reaches up and slices Frenchy's ear with the razor.

                FRENCHY
    He'll be glad to hear that.

Dixie and Frenchy exit.

118C INT - MADDEN'S OFFICE - NIGHT:  <u>FRENCHY GIVES WATCH</u>

Madden is sitting at his desk, as Frenchy walks in.

                MADDEN
    You okay?

Madden gets up, looks him over.

                FRENCHY
    I'm fine.

                MADDEN
    Did you get home?

                FRENCHY
    Yeah.  Changed clothes,
    cleaned up.

                MADDEN
    They hurt you?

                FRENCHY
    Nah.  Treated me like a
    king.

                    MADDEN
          What happened to your ear?

                    FRENCHY
          Oh this?  Playing tennis with
          Mad Dog Dwyer.

                    MADDEN
          Tennis?

                    FRENCHY
          Yeah, he hit a ball over my
          head... I raced back to get
          it and crashed into the metal
          fence.  Cut my ear.

                    MADDEN
          You were playing tennis with him?

                    FRENCHY
          Yeah.  He gave me drinks, good
          food.  The place was nice, well
          furnished.

                    MADDEN
          What was he trying to do?  Kill
          you with kindness?  I was worried
          sick about you.

X118 INT - BAMVILLE CLUB - NIGHT:    SANDMAN/CLAY REUNION

   Sandman enters and is seated at ringside.  The band is
   playing, and Clay is just starting "Crazy Rhythm."  Clay
   sees Sandman and stops singing.

                    CLAY
          Ladies and gentlemen, a big
          star has just come into the
          club.  Sandman Williams, my
          brother.

Sandman gets up, takes bow, looks at Clay.

                    SANDMAN
          Clay Williams, the finest tap
          dancer in Harlem.

Bumpy stands up.

                    BUMPY
          Dalbert, why don't you and your
          brother Clayton dance together?

Audience applauds. Madame St. Clair is seated near bar.

> MADAME ST. CLAIR
> Yes, dance, Sandman, dance.

Sandman joins Clay on dance floor.

> SANDMAN
> You wanna finish out "Crazy
> Rhythm"?

Clay looks to bandleader and nods, and the brothers go into the number. At the end, they embrace to great applause.

118C INT - MADDEN'S OFFICE - NIGHT: <u>FRENCHY GIVES WATCH</u>

Madden and Frenchy.

> FRENCHY
> How long was I gone? Let
> me see your watch.

Madden hands him pocket watch.

> FRENCHY
> Let's see, he picked me up
> in front of the club about...

He drops the watch.

> FRENCHY
> Oh, shit, sorry.... I think
> I broke it.

> MADDEN
> Give it to me.

> FRENCHY
> No, no no. I can fix it.
> Here.

He puts watch on desk, picks up sculpture and slams it down on watch, smashing it.

> FRENCHY
> You cheap son of a bitch!
> You only offered five hundred
> dollars for me!

Madden is stunned.

> MADDEN
> What?!

                    FRENCHY
          If you were kidnapped, I
          wouldn't offer more than that
          for you?

                    MADDEN
          Five hundred dollars?

                    FRENCHY
          That's what I heard.

                    MADDEN
          Fifty grand I paid for you!
          Fifty grand! He only wanted
          thirty-five grand. I gave him
          fifty not to hurt you. Five
          hundred dollars. I would've
          given five hundred thousand
          dollars. I was worried sick
          about you.

Frenchy is silent.

                    MADDEN
          Shit. Look what you did to
          my fuckin' watch.

                    FRENCHY
          Fifty grand?

                    MADDEN
          Yeah.

Madden's broken watch is dangling from his chain. Frenchy
pulls a small package out of his pocket, hands it to Madden.

                    MADDEN
          What's this?

Frenchy turns away. Madden opens the package.

                    MADDEN
          A platinum watch.
               (pause)
          You asshole.

They look at each other for a moment, embrace, exit.

118A EXT - DRUGSTORE - NIGHT:   <u>VINCE ENTERS DRUGSTORE</u>

Vince hurries across to drugstore. There is a "Mob Boss"
poster out front. A car pulls up, parks, two men get out.

118D  INT - DRUGSTORE - NIGHT:   <u>VINCE KILLED IN DRUGSTORE</u>

Vince goes to phone booth, phone rings.  Vince enters.

                    VINCE
        Hello -- hello, oh, yeah,
        sure...(etc.)

The two men enter the store.  From under raincoat one of the latter reveals a machine gun.  His associate calms patron and owner of store.  Man with machine gun opens fire, catches Vince in phone booth.  Patsy comes in, screaming.

CLOSE UP -- The dangling receiver.

118F  INT - MADDEN'S OFFICE - NIGHT:   <u>MADDEN HANGS UP PHONE</u>

CLOSE VIEW

Madden hangs up the phone, continues to draw horses.

118G  CLOSE ON "Mob Boss" poster, front page stories of Variety, other entertainment papers.

"Dixie Dwyer A Rising Star in Gangland Movie"
"Brother of Mad Dog Dwyer Playing Gang Boss"
"A Tale of Two Brothers: Vincent the Killer,
 Dixie the Actor"
"Sandman Williams Star of New Cotton Club Revue"

"Hi-De-Ho" echoing.

                    TED HUSING o.s.
        This program is coming to you
        live...

                                    DISSOLVE:

140  INT - COTTON CLUB - NIGHT:   <u>COTTON CLUB II</u>

CLOSE on TED HUSING.

                    HUSING
        ...from the Cotton Club in
        Harlem, New York City.  Now
        Cab Calloway, the prince of
        Hi-De-Ho, will entertain you
        with "Minnie the Moocher."

PAN to CAB CALLOWAY and his band doing "Minnie the Moocher."

141  EXT - COTTON CLUB - NIGHT:   <u>LILA PASSES WITH CHAPLIN</u>

Lila Rose has arrived on the arm of Charlie Chaplin, whom somebody recognizes. Charlie does his little Tramp's walk for gawkers. Lila Rose confronts Holmes the doorman square in the eye and he recognizes her. He says nothing, doesn't stop her. He smiles. As she passes:

>              HOLMES
>     You lookin' mighty good
>     tonight, pretty lady.

Dramatic VIEW on Lila Rose as she passes up the stairs.

141A  EXT - LENOX AVENUE - NIGHT:   <u>WINNIE LATE FOR SHOW</u>

Norma and Winnie are hurrying along. Winnie looks very childlike in her absence of makeup, and kid clothes.

>              NORMA
>     I am so upset with you. Where
>     you been when you should be
>     gettin' ready?
>
>              WINNIE
>     Let it go, Mama.
>
>              NORMA
>     You were with that Bumpy Rhodes
>     is what I think. That's a
>     gangster, girl. That's wrong,
>     wrong, wrong.
>
>              WINNIE
>     Please let it go, Mama.

They approach the back entrance of Cotton Club, and enter past Joe, the doorman.

>              JOE
>     Welcome to the Cotton Club,
>     ladies.

142  INT - COTTON CLUB - NIGHT

Dixie enters the Cotton Club alone and gets all of the fanfare and welcome accorded Gloria Swanson. Kid Griffin shows him to his table, people ask for autographs.

Madden, Frenchy come to greet LUCIANO. Kid Griffin seats him. The three gangsters draw the curtains on booth.

Vera is with Dutch and Abbadabba that night. She is a sophisticate with her own crowd of cronies, flacks and yes-men, known for her humor, and as Dutch's infamous mistress. Bumpy arrives with black hoods, greets Dixie and is seated.

143 INT - BACKSTAGE - NIGHT

Winnie's first show, Norma is there. Sandman is big star, all the girls flirt with him, as they get ready to go on.

144 VIEW ON THE REVUE

"Doin' the New Lowdown." Sandman and the girls. Chaplin and Lila enter, sit down.

VIEW ON BUMPY

Watching Winnie perform.

Madame St. Clair enters, very grandly, passes Schultz table. She and Dutch make eye contact. Contempt and venom. She moves past without speaking and goes to Bumpy's table. Madame St. Clair sits down. She can't get Bumpy's attention beyond a brief nod. Bumpy only has eyes for Winnie.

>        MADAME ST. CLAIR
>            (wryly)
>        There is something attractive
>        about youth.

"Doin' the New Low Down" ends. Bumpy goes backstage.

145 VIEW ON THE REVUE

"Lady With the Fan" begins.

VIEW ON LUCIANO'S BOOTH

Luciano, Madden and Frenchy. The curtains are closed. Luciano peeks through curtains, sees Dutch.

>        LUCIANO
>    So that's the Dutchman, huh.
>    If something isn't done about
>    that maniac, this new special
>    prosecutor, Dewey, will indict
>    us all.
>
>        MADDEN
>    Dutch has moved fast in Harlem.

                    LUCIANO
          His rackets are very appealing.

                    FRENCHY
          Mr. Luciano. I wouldn't take
          the Dutchman too lightly.

                    LUCIANO
          But does he have real balls?

                    MADDEN
          Well, now that his yid is
          dead, we'll find out.

                    LUCIANO
          And then we'll divide his
          Harlem rackets with everyone
          in the family.

Frenchy and Madden look at each other, as Luciano opens curtains to see "Lady With the Fan." Madden and Frenchy exit.

VIEW ON DUTCH'S TABLE

Vera, Abbadabba, Dutch talking, Kid Griffin comes by.

                    GRIFFIN
          A call for you, Mr. Schultz.
          They said it was urgent.

Dutch follows Griffin.

146  VIEW INTO THE RESERVATION ROOM

Dutch is on the phone.

                    FRANCES
          Save it for your girlfriend,
          Arthur. This is your wife.

                    DUTCH
          I'm not here -- would you let
          me explain?

                    FRANCES
          I'll see you in a wink,
          four-flusher.

She hangs up. Dutch looks at receiver, hangs up, exits quickly. As he walks to his table, he greets BABE RUTH. The "Nicholas Brothers" come on.

147  INT - BACKSTAGE - NIGHT

Bumpy looks for Winnie, finds her and they make eye contact. Winnie shakes her head, gestures at him to get out, he's not supposed to be here. He moves toward her. Behind him his two bodyguards follow but keep their distance, watching. About center backstage Bumpy and Winnie come together.

WINNIE
They won't let you back here.

BUMPY
I'm already here. Never mind nobody else, just meet me after the show and we'll go someplace.

WINNIE
I can't no more, Bumpy. The family's clampin' down on me. They know you're married.

BUMPY
Everybody knows that.

Mike Best comes out of musical instruments room (?) and sees Bumpy but doesn't see his two henchmen. He goes to Bumpy.

BEST
Who are you and whataya doin' here?

BUMPY
I'm talking to my friend, Winnie. Who are _you_ and what are _you_ doin' interrupting me?

BEST
Another uppity nigger.

He lays hands on Bumpy. Sandman is coming down from dressing room as this happens. Bumpy's bodyguards flash across the stage to help Bumpy. One finds a stage pin, gets necklock on Best with pin while his partner twists Best's arm. Bumpy is free, Best immobilized, silenced.

No screaming, just sudden silence, total focus by all performers. Other hoods may get wind of this and come to Best's rescue, and Bumpy instinctively knows this. He moves into toilet gesturing to bring Best in. They gag him, and Bumpy dunks his head in toilet bowl.

> BUMPY
> (after first dunk)
> This uppity nigger is buyin'
> you a drink.

Sandman comes in and is very excited. He likes the position Best is in, smiles, then frowns his concern for Bumpy.

> BUMPY
> This drink is for my friend
> Sandman, for what you did
> to him.

Bumpy dunks Best one more time.

> BUMPY
> One for the road... that bumpy,
> bumpy road.

146  INT - COTTON CLUB - NIGHT

VIEW ON DUTCH'S TABLE

Dutch sits down, face showing confusion, frustration.

> ABBADABBA
> Everything all right, boss?

> DUTCH
> It was Frances.

He looks at Vera.

> DUTCH
> You can't be here with me
> if she's comin'.

> VERA
> You want me to disappear?

She shakes her head, incredulous.

> VERA
> You're really afraid of her.

> DUTCH
> Vera, it's my wife, for chrissake.

> VERA
> You're afraid of your wife.

146A INT - BACKSTAGE - NIGHT

Norma is helping Winnie with her costume after the event with Bumpy and Best.

>			NORMA
>	You better stay outa trouble
>	with gangsters, honey, if
>	you wanna keep your job.
>	You're the first dark-skinned
>	girl in this show. You know
>	how many like you in those
>	breadlines today?

150 INT - COTTON CLUB STAIRS - NIGHT

Frances comes up stairs, shoves aside a couple just reaching top. She's at full throttle. We hear "Barbecue Bess" o.s.

149 INT - COTTON CLUB - NIGHT

CLOSE on "Barbecue Bess" in a risque song.

VIEW ON MADDEN'S TABLE

>			FRENCHY
>		(mockingly)
>	Some tough guy, this Dutchman.
>
>			MADDEN
>	Tough he never was, just crazy.
>	Remember Joe Flynn?
>
>			FRENCHY
>	Now he wants to kill the
>	prosecutor, Dewey.
>
>			MADDEN
>	Yeah, that's what he says.
>
>			FRENCHY
>	Lepke says it can be done.
>	But then we'd all fry for it.
>		(pause) Dewey is a big one.
>
>			MADDEN
>	You're right. That stupid
>	bastard won't take no
>	for answer.

"Barbecue Bess" ends, "Jitterbug" comes on.

VIEW ON LUCIANO'S TABLE.

Dark Italian, TRIGGER MIKE COPPOLA, approaches Luciano. They embrace, speak in Italian.

                  MONK
     Trigger Mike Coppola just
     come in to see Charlie.

                MADDEN
     Undertaker time.

Coppola embraces Luciano and sits at his booth. Frances arrives. Kid Griffin confronts her.

                FRANCES
     I know exactly where I'm going.

She strides past the Kid, goes directly to Dutch's table. She screams -- getting everyone's attention.

                FRANCES
     I knew she was with you.

                DUTCH
     Frances...

                FRANCES
     You're such a rotten liar,
     Arthur.

She shoves Vera back into her seat.

                FRANCES
     Sit down. (to Dutch) I just
     wanted to show you how
     transparent you really are.

During this, Vera has stood again and roughly shoved her way past Frances, moving quickly to Dixie's table.

                VERA
     Is this seat taken?

                DIXIE
     No, no, I was waiting for a
     beautiful woman to sit down
     and fall in love with me.

                VERA
     I already did that.

                    DIXIE
          There's no law against doing
          it twice.

Back at Dutch's table.

                    DUTCH
          Frances, you got it all wrong...

                    FRANCES
          Don't think I'm gonna stand
          around and wait forever while
          you show her all over town.

She slaps Dutch, then abruptly leaves and goes to Vera and
Dixie's table. In her wake, she pulls the tablecloth and
its contents onto the floor.

                    DUTCH
          Frances! For chrissake!

He views the devastation and a lot of money on the floor.

                    DUTCH
          Will you get the money, for
          chrissake.

VIEW ON DIXIE'S TABLE

                    VERA
          Watch out, she's coming.

Frances holds her fingernails close to Vera's face.

                    FRANCES
          Here's five good reasons why
          you should fold up your legs
          and go home...

She feints with nails, doesn't scratch. Dixie restrains
her.

                    FRANCES
          I'm not afraid of you, get
          out of my way.

Dutch comes rushing over and accosts Dixie.

                    DUTCH
          Keep your hands off my wife.

FRANCES
(to Dixie)
I'm surprised at you.  I thought
you got out from under his thumb.
See you in the movies, lover boy.

DIXIE
Yeah, see you around.

Frances takes off toward the exit, towing off another
tablecloth and contents in her wake.

DUTCH
(going after Frances)
Frances, Frances...

Vera walks away in the other direction.  Dixie follows.

DIXIE
Did she stab you with those nails?

VERA
Damn near it.  She ought to be
put away.  What I'd like to do
is rip off her lips.

DIXIE
Hoodlums are bad news, but
married hoodlums are worse.
How's it feel being the other
woman?

VERA
How's it feel being the other man?

DIXIE
(stopping her)
Listen, I don't do that anymore.
What's mine is mine, nobody else's.
That's the way it is, see?

VERA
You see?  What, are you out from
under his thumb now or something?

DIXIE
Yeah, yeah, didn't you hear?
I'm the Mob Boss now.

He starts moving her towards kitchen door.

VERA
Where are you taking me?

DIXIE
Someplace we can be alone.


152 INT - BACKSTAGE - NIGHT

Dixie can't find quiet corner. He sees opening between stage curtains, takes Vera by hand, and moves between curtains.

VERA
How'd you get out so fast, so easy? Movie star, and you got it all.

DIXIE
What about you? You're this famous comedienne, now you got your own club, and the little girl's not even twenty yet.

VERA
Yeah, but look what she had to do to get it.

DIXIE
You could have come with me, you know.

VERA
I wouldn't go any place on a shoe string. I've been making my own way since I was thirteen...

Vera starts to break down, romance on back burner.

VERA
Money's the only thing that ever saves you.

DIXIE
Hey, you're wrong. You're very wrong.

VERA
It's all that saved me. Money and my looks. I was born looking eighteen.

DIXIE
I can save you.

VERA
No you can't.

                    DIXIE
            Try me.

                    VERA
                (crying)
            You can't.

He holds her as she sobs into his shoulder, then she
straightens up, wilfully pulls herself together, faces him.

                    VERA
            You don't know what it's like
            being his slave. He's everywhere.
            I got my own club but I can't
            breathe in it.

Backstage, outside the curtains, Herman Stark sees Dixie's
and Vera's feet. He moves up to curtain.

                    STARK
            You go on in about two minutes.
            And the Dutchman is looking for
            the lady.

                    VERA
                (to Dixie)
            You see what I mean? It was
            great while it lasted.

They kiss again, and exit.


153  INT - COTTON CLUB - NIGHT

     VIEW ON DUTCH'S TABLE

     Vera, hostile to Dutch, glowers as Stark introduces Dixie.

     VIEW ON STARK

                    STARK
            What a night, what a mob, what a
            crowd. Ladies and gentlemen,
            it's Celebrity Night this
            evening. That's right, the
            stars come out. And tonight we
            have the man who has become
            America's favorite gangster,
            starring in the movie that's
            sweeping the country, "Mob
            Boss." And he's back in Harlem
                        (MORE)

                    STARK contd.
          doing what he always does when
          he gets the chance --playing his
          cornet.  Tonight is a special
          night and it's a first.  Tonight
          we have the first white musician
          to sit in with the Cotton Club
          orchestra.  So, ladies and
          gentlemen, put your hands
          together, give a warm round of
          applause to Harlem's own Dixie
          Dwyer!

Dixie comes with horn, climbs into seat on stand, plays.

VIEW ON DUTCH'S TABLE

                    DUTCH
               (mocking)
          "Mob Boss."  The punk's a
          marshmallow.  All he did
          was copy my style.

                    VERA
          You got about as much style
          as a bowl of turnips.

                    DUTCH
          Ah, shut up and have a drink.

                    VERA
          I don't want a drink.

                    DUTCH
          Drink.

                    VERA
          Drinkers lie and I want
          to tell the truth.

Dutch looks at her, then looks back at Dixie, snorts his
contempt, then again looks back to Vera.

                    DUTCH
          What do you want to tell the
          truth about?

                    VERA
          I don't know.

                    DUTCH
          What were you doin' backstage
          with that punk?

                    VERA
          I was kissing him.

Dutch gets furious, but he's not sure what to do about it.
He doesn't know if it's true, or another of her jokes.

VIEW ON DIXIE

Doing his solo.

VIEW ON VERA

                    VERA
          I love him, I always have.

                    DUTCH
          Did you ever sleep with him?

                    VERA
          Whenever I got the chance.
            (pause)  And I will again,
          if I get the chance.

Dutch stares briefly, venom in his eyes, then leans over,
grabs her hair, shakes her.  Dixie has finished playing.  He
walks quickly across stage towards Dutch and Vera.

                    DUTCH
          You'll never get it.

He takes off her bracelet, earring, cutting her.  She
winces.  On stage, the spotlight has come on Sandman,
beginning "Copper Colored Gal."  Dixie approaches them.

                    DIXIE
          Take your hands off her,
          scumbones.  Don't you ever
          touch her like that again.

                    DUTCH
          You son of a bitch.  I'll rip
          your balls off.

Various bodyguards and henchmen sense violence about to
erupt, and move toward Dutch and Dixie.  We sense these
men's fingers are inching toward their triggers.

VIEW ON SANDMAN

Singing to girls.  He notices trouble.

                    VERA
          Don't get into it, Dixie.

                    DIXIE
          I'm in it as much as you.
                (to Dutch)
          Whataya want, to run everybody's
          life forever?  You wanna be
          Genghis Khan for chrissake?
          You get into people's lives
          and you just turn them to shit.
                (whispers, hard)  Whataya
          gonna do, cut out our hearts
          like you did Joe Flynn?  How
          many people can you kill, Dutch?

Big Frenchy moves in and other of Madden's mob are on the
periphery, Mike Best, Monk, others.

                    FRENCHY
          Take it outside, boys.  No
          trouble in the club.

Madden mobsters nudge Abbadabba and Dutch's other bodyguard
toward the door, their women moving with them.

                    DUTCH
                (to Vera)
          Let's go.

                    VERA
          I'm not going anyplace with
          you, not any more.

                    DUTCH
          I said let's go.

Dixie moves between Dutch and Vera.

                    DIXIE
          Crawl back inyo your rat hole
          and leave the girl alone.

Dutch walks off, then explodes, just as he did with Joe
Flynn.  He pulls gun from shoulder holster, points it at
Dixie.

CLOSE ON THE GUN

We SEE Sandman and the girls dancing the end of "Copper
Colored Gal."

CLOSE on Dixie, Madden, Frenchy, and the gun which is being
cocked as Dutch pulls trigger.  Sandman kicks gun out of his
hand and it goes flying.  Shot fired by the gun and people
scream.

VIEW ON THE WINDOW

The gun flies through.  Dutch is manhandled by Madden's boys.

153A EXT - COTTON CLUB - NIGHT

The gun falls by Holmes, who looks upward.

154 INT - COTTON CLUB - NIGHT

Pandemonium.

>            DUTCH
> You fuckin' micks, you'll all
> die!

Abbadabba tries to fight way back to Dutch and is thrown down the stairs by Monk.  Screams and curses but Dutch's people are outnumbered and disarmed.

155 VIEW ON CLUB

Stark is trying to restore order.

155A EXT - COTTON CLUB - NIGHT

Dutch, Abbadabba, and other bodyguard and women move down street to car and pile in.  Madden's guns trained on them.

154B VIEW ON LUCIANO'S BOOTH

VIEW ON LUCIANO, MADDEN, COPPOLA, ETC.

>           LUCIANO
>         (darkly)
> Got a phone?
>
>           MADDEN
> Use my office.

They move into the office.

A156 INT - CAR - NIGHT:  <u>CONSPIRE IN CAR</u>

Dutch and Abbadabba conspiring.

                        DUTCH
            I still say he oughta be hit.
            Maybe I won't hire anybody.
            It'd be a pleasure to blast
            him myself.

155B INT - COTTON CLUB - NIGHT

MEDIUM VIEW ON SANDMAN

Spotlight snaps on. Tremendous applause. He begins a tap
dance improvisation, with no band. There is so much
applause and whistling, that several fights break out over
the noise ruining Sandman's taps. Finally, it becomes
silent, and we hear the taps.

INTERCUT WITH TAP SOLO:

157 INT - COTTON CLUB - NIGHT

CLOSE SHOT

Lucky Luciano, getting wine bottle.

146 INT - PALACE CHOP HOUSE - NIGHT: <u>DUTCH AT CHOP HOUSE</u>

Dutch, Abbadabba, two other gangsters eat and drink at table
in corner.

                        ABBADABBA
            ...Last time you did somebody
            yourself it cost you 25 G's.
            I don't like it.

                        DUTCH
            You don't have to.
                 (getting up)
            I gotta take a leak and
            go get some sleep.

He puts on light topcoat, grey fedora, goes to men's room.

Two men, CHARLIE "THE BUG" WORKMAN and MENDY WEISS enter.
The Bug glances at the bar, sees bartender and a couple of
customers. No one pays any attention to him.

As he walks toward men's room he turns .38 caliber pistol on
trio in corner, firing across room while Weiss sweeps table
with tommy gun brought in under his coat.

156A INT - COTTON CLUB - NIGHT

   Luciano pops cork himself.

158B INT - PALACE CHOP HOUSE - NIGHT:  <u>ABBA KILLED</u>

   Flying slugs shatter cigarette machine and display bottles, smash into front window and splinter wall over front entrance. Abbadabba tumbles to tile floor in a pool of blood, moaning.

159 VIEW IN MEN'S ROOM:  <u>DUTCH KILLED</u>

   The Bug kicks open men's room door. As Dutch turns and sees him he grabs for his gun, but it is too late. The Bug fires, sending a bullet through Schultz' left side. A second bullet misses and smashes into the peeling wall over urinal and The Bug whirls out door.

   SANDMAN'S TAP SOLO -- RAPID LIKE A MACHINE GUN

   Dutch clutches his right side and steps forward out of men's room, reeling like he is intoxicated. He goes over to a table and puts left hand on it to steady himself and then plops into a chair. His head bounces on the table.

160 INT - COTTON CLUB - NIGHT

   VIEW ON LUCIANO -- He pours red wine.

                    LUCIANO
         Salud.

                    MADDEN
         Salood.

They toast.

164 VIEW ON CHAPLIN TABLE

   Sandman's solo ends. Lila Rose excuses herself from table, goes backstage.

165 INT - BACKSTAGE - NIGHT

   Sandman takes Lila Rose to a corner.

                    SANDMAN
          So, are you white now or are
          you black?

                    LILA ROSE
          Well, my mother's white and
          my father's colored so what
          color does that make me?

                    SANDMAN
          You're driving me crazy, Lila.
          How about a late night supper?

                    LILA ROSE
          You might be able to talk me
          into that.

                    SANDMAN
          Tell me one more thing, Lila.
          Do you love me?

                    LILA ROSE
          I adore you.

                    SANDMAN
          Good.  Let's get married instead
          of havin' dinner.

                    LILA ROSE
          You might be able to talk
          me into that.

     They kiss.

163  VIEW ON MADDEN'S TABLE

     Vera and Dixie are leaving.  Luciano comes up to them.  They
     walk together, approaching Madden.

                    LUCIANO
          I liked your picture.  You
          make a good lookin' mob boss.
          I like it when the mob boss
          is good lookin'.

                    DIXIE
          You mean like Owney here.

     This gets a laugh.  Vera and Dixie continue on their way.

                    MADDEN
          You know I'm not gonna boss
          nothing after next week, Charlie.

LUCIANO
You retiring?

MADDEN
I'm going back to jail. Just a little parole violation but it's not a bad excuse to get out of this racket. There's a lot of ambition in the rackets these days, you know what I mean, Charlie? The Irish don't always know when to quit, but some of us learn as we go.

166 Sandman and Lila Rose approach Chaplin table. Ad lib congratulations to Sandman on his dance.

CHAPLIN
We're all going over to Small's Paradise for their next show. Won't you join us?

SANDMAN
I was thinkin' of puttin' on a show of my own if I found the right audience.

LILA ROSE
He found an audience. We're gettin' married in half an hour.

CHAPLIN
I never argue with romance.

Sandman and Lila Rose kiss, he takes her off.

166A EXT - HARLEM STREET - NIGHT: <u>VERA/DIXIE FAREWELL</u>

Vera and Dixie together, maybe half an hour after pandemonium. He has a car, so has she. Wind blows.

VERA
You were very brave. So many times you've been my protector.

DIXIE
I could make a career out of it.

VERA
It wouldn't work. He'll never let me go.

                    DIXIE
          That part of your life is over.

                    VERA
          We'd spend the rest of our
          lives not answering the doorbell.

                    DIXIE
          He wouldn't kill me.  Gangsters
          don't kill celebrities.

She laughs and they kiss, she pulls away.

                    VERA
          And whores make lousy wives.

                    DIXIE
          Who said you were a whore?  And
          who asked you to get married?

                    VERA
          I could never live with
          anybody for very long.

                    DIXIE
          Ten years and we'll call it
          quits.  What's more it's a
          nice ride.  I got a parlor
          car all to myself.

                    VERA
          You goin' someplace?

                    DIXIE
          Goin' west, young lady.  I'm
          gonna ask you one more time.
          You wanna come along?

He stops, looks at her, wants yes for an answer.

                    VERA
          No, Dix.  I love you, I love
          you truly, but no.  Take the
          little girl out of New York
          and who is she?

                    DIXIE
          She'd be a star in any town.
          Even Albany.  (pause) Now
          I'm gonna leave you, Vera as
          in Very Very.  I'm not going
          to kiss you any more.  Not even
                    (MORE)

                    DIXIE contd.
          gonna listen to any more of
          your jokes.  (pause) That's
          maybe the saddest thing I've
          ever said to anybody.

Vera chokes up, embraces him.

                    VERA
          Flies in my brain.  They
          never never never go away.

                    DIXIE
          I'll miss you like I never
          missed any woman in this
          world before.

                    VERA
          Do me the biggest favor you ever
          did for me, will you, kiddo?
          Kiss me on my lovely lips and
          don't say anything.  Just keep
          looking over your shoulder and
          maybe one day we'll see each
          other again and maybe we'll have
          a drink and maybe we'll make
          love.  Maybe, Dixie, my very
          very lover.  Maybe.

They clinch, go to their separate cars.

167 INT - COTTON CLUB - NIGHT:  <u>DAYBREAK EXPRESS</u>

Orchestra breaks into Ellington number, "Daybreak Express."
Set pieces indicate Grand Central Station, Track #3, Gate
#5, etc.  Brightly uniformed porters leap over luggage.

168 INT - GRAND CENTRAL STATION - NIGHT:  <u>GRAND CENTRAL</u>

Frenchy and Madden walking across Grand Central Station
towards FEDERAL OFFICERS waiting on platform.

                    MADDEN
          Have you fixed the warden?

                    FRENCHY
          It's done.

                    MADDEN
          Did you get the wall to wall
          carpeting?

                                FRENCHY
                    After the way we got Sing Sing
                    set up for you -- parole in
                    three months and the horse
                    farm in Arkansas could be a
                    letdown when you get out.

    A quick embrace, then Madden is quickly whisked off.

                                MADDEN
                    Bring the new Cotton Club
                    show up to Sing Sing.

                                FRENCHY
                    Week from Wednesday.

                                MADDEN
                    I'll get 'em started on the
                    scenery.

    Vera waits for Dixie with 16 pieces of matched leather
    luggage. He arrives, holding a bottle of champagne. Dixie
    takes Vera to the "Hollywood Special," his private car.

171 Frances, dressed in mourning, precedes Dutch's coffin
    carried to gate #3.

172 Sandman and Lila Rose run to go on their honeymoon, followed
    by friends and kids in the show. They throw rice.

173 EXT - OBSERVATION PLATFORM - NIGHT

    Dixie opens champagne, offers Vera a glass.

                                DIXIE
                    Drink before you make love,
                    Vera Cicero.

    They pull away.

174 INT - COTTON CLUB - NIGHT

    BIG FINALE. The Cotton Club company bows.

                                            LIGHTS DOWN:


                                THE END

# CONTINUITY

| Sc. #/Sc. | | Page # |
|---|---|---|
| 1 | HARLEM HISTORY MONTAGE<br>(Ext - Harlem - Day) | 1 |
| 2 | DIXIE POV COTTON CLUB<br>(Ext - Cotton Club - Night) | 2 |
| 19 | SANDMAN ON NUMBERS BEAT<br>(Ext - Lenox Ave. - Night) | 3 |
| 2A | SANDMAN PAYS OFF DIXIE<br>(Ext - Cotton Club - Night) | 3 |
| 3 | BAMVILLE BOMB<br>(Ext/Int Bamville Club - Night) | 4 |
| 4 | ENTER VERA'S AFTER BOMB<br>(Ext - Vera's Apt. - Night) | 9 |
| 5 | DIXIE PUTS VERA TO BED<br>(Int - Vera's Apt. - Night) | 8 |
| 6 | SANDMAN WAKES UP<br>(Int - Sandman's Bedroom - Day) | 9 |
| 7 | WILLIAMS DISCUSS BOMB<br>(Int - Williams Apt. - Day) | 9 |
| 8 | DIXIE/VINCE DISCUSS BOMB<br>(Int - Luncheonette - Day) | 10 |
| 9 | DUTCH NEEDS APES<br>(Ext - Street - Day) | 10 |
| 10 | WINNIE PRACTICES STEP<br>(Int - Williams Apt. - Day) | 11 |
| 11-12 | BROTHERS CROSS<br>(Ext - Street - Day) | 12 |
| 13 | VINCE SAYS HE'S MARRIED<br>(Ext - Dwyer Apt. - Day) | 13 |
| 14-16 | TISH WELCOMES DIXIE HOME<br>(Int - Dwyer Apt. - Day) | 13 |
| 17 | EXIT AUDITION/SEE LILA ROSE<br>(Ext - Cotton Club - Day) | 16 |

| Sc. #/Sc. | | Page # |
|---|---|---|
| 18 | SANDMAN/STARK ON STAIRS<br>(Int - Cotton Club Stairs - Day) | 17 |
| 19A | SANDMAN WATCHES GIRLS REHEARSAL<br>(Int - Cotton Club - Day) | 17 |
| 21 | SOL APPROACHES DIXIE<br>(Int - Jazz Speakeasy - Day) | 17 |
| A22 | CAR DRIVES BY<br>(Ext - Street - Night) | 18 |
| 22 | DIXIE/SOL DRIVE TO HOTEL<br>(Int - Car - Night) | 19 |
| 23 | DIXIE & SOL CORRIDOR<br>(Int - Hotel Corridor - Night) | 19 |
| 24 | DUTCH TELLS DIXIE ABOUT VERA<br>(Int - Suite #1 - Night) | 19 |
| 24A | VERA ELEVATOR<br>(Int - Hotel Elevator - Night) | 20 |
| 24C | DIXIE SEES VERA<br>(Int - Suite #1 - Night) | 20 |
| 26 | PEACE CONFERENCE BEGINS<br>(Int - Suite #2 - Night) | 21 |
| 27 | YOU SURE ARE LOW-DOWN<br>(Int - Suite #1 - Night) | 21 |
| 27A | KISS IN BATHROOM<br>(Int - Bathroom - Night) | 22 |
| 28 | PEACE CONFERENCE CONCLUDES<br>(Int - Suite #2 - Night) | 22 |
| 30 | VERA SINGS, DIXIE PLAYS<br>(Int - Suite #1 - Night) | 23 |
| 31 | JOE FLYNN MURDER<br>(Int - Suite #3 - Night) | 25 |
| 31A | DRIVING FAST AFTER MURDER<br>(Ext - Street/Dusenberg - Night) | 27 |

| Sc. #/Sc. | | Page # |
|---|---|---|
| 32 | DRIVE HOME AFTER MURDER<br>(Int - Car - Night) | 27 |
| 33 | DUTCH INTO SHADOWS<br>(Ext - House - Night) | 28 |
| 34 | DIXIE & VERA DISCUSS MURDER<br>(Int - Car - Night) | 29 |
| 36 | DROP OFF VERA<br>(Ext - Vera's Apt. - Night) | 29 |

37-68: <u>COTTON CLUB I</u>

| | | |
|---|---|---|
| 38 | Entertainers enter | 29 |
| 37 | Patrons enter | 30 |
| 39 | Backstage preparations | 30 |
| 43 | Kitchen preparations | 30 |
| 43A | Patrons up stairs | 30 |
| 40 | Dwyers arrive C.C. | 30 |
| 41 | Dwyers go up stairs | 30 |
| 44 | Dwyers see interior | 31 |
| 45 | White Heat | 31 |
| 46 | Dwyers get poor table/ meet Madden | 31 |
| 47 | Berry Brothers | 32 |
| 42 | Ready Aim Fire | 32 |
| 42A | Peters Sisters, Rhythm Queens | 33 |
| 47B | Men's Room | 33 |
| A62 | Williams backstage, watching | 34 |
| 48 | Shake That Thing | 34 |
| 63 | Sandman watches show | 34 |
| 64 | POV Lila Rose (Creole Love Call) | 34 |
| 48A | Dutch and Frances arrive | 34 |
| 49 | Frenchy sees Dutch | 35 |
| 51 | Dutch/Frances at table | 35 |
| 50 | Frenchy tells Madden | 35 |
| 51 | Frenchy tells Dutch | 36 |
| 53 | Death Yiddish style | 36 |
| 53A | One Man Dance, up stairs | 37 |
| 50A | Gloria Swanson arrives | 37 |
| 58 | Madden & Dutch on roof | 37 |
| 58A | Revue (Butterbeans & Susie) | 38 |
| 61 | Sandman wants to marry Lila | 38 |
| A59 | Revue (Creole Rhapsody) | 39 |
| 59 | Dixie/Vera talking | 39 |
| 54 | Williams Brothers | 39 |
| 56 | The Mooche | 40 |
| 57 | Dance intermission | 40 |
| 60 | Dutch offers Dixie job | 43 |

| Sc. #/Sc. | | Page # |
|---|---|---|
| 52 | Mike Best shoves Sandman | 43 |
| 66 | Dixie meets Swanson | 44 |
| 67 | Lila gets mad | 44 |
| 67A | Entertainers leaving | 44 |
| 67B | Patrons leaving | 45 |
| 69 | COMMUNITY REHEARSAL (Tall Tan Terrific)<br>(Int - Church Stage - Day) | 45 |
| 71 | HOOFERS CLUB DANCE<br>(Int - Hoofers Club - Day) | 46 |
| 72 | SUGAR REMINDS SANDMAN HE'S LATE<br>(Int - Hoofers Club - Day) | 46 |
| 73 | SANDMAN RUNS DOWN STREET<br>(Ext - Street - Day) | 47 |
| 74 | SANDMAN RUNS THRU BAR<br>(Int - Bar - Day) | 47 |
| 75 | SANDMAN LATE WITH NUMBERS<br>(Int - Numbers Bank - Day) | 48 |
| 76 | WINNIE SAYS BUMPY LIKES HER<br>(Ext - Street - Day) | 49 |
| 76A | ABBA EXPLAINS #/DIXIE SERVITUDE<br>(Int - Palace Chop House - Day) | 49 |
| A76 | PICK UP LAUNDRY<br>(Ext - Palace Chop House - Day) | 52 |
| 76B | DIXIE ENTERS C.C.<br>(Ext - Cotton Club - Day) | 52 |
| 76C | DIXIE MEETS WITH MADDEN<br>(Int - C.C. Stairs - Day) | 53 |
| 76D | DIXIE CLOSES LIMO DOOR<br>(Ext - Cotton Club - Day) | 54 |
| 100 | DIXIE BUYS APPLE<br>(Ext - Street - Night) | 54 |
| 102 | DIXIE SEES VINCE WOUNDED<br>(Int - Car - Night) | 54 |

| Sc. #/Sc. | | Page # |
|---|---|---|
| 124 | SANDMAN AND CLAY BREAK UP<br>(Int - Backstage - Day) | 55 |
| 102A | MONTAGE VINCE/DIXIE | 56 |
| 136 | SCREENTEST<br>(Int - Screening Room - Day) | 56 |
| 86 | TAXI PICKS UP VERA<br>(Ext - Vera's Apt. - Night) | 56 |
| 87 | DRIVE VERA TO BAMVILLE<br>(Int - Dusenberg - Night) | 56 |
| 88 | YOU LOOK TERRIBLE<br>(Int - Bamville Club - Night) | 57 |
| 89 | SOL LOOKS IN BAMVILLE<br>(Ext - Bamville Club - Night) | 58 |
| 93 | LOOK AT ME TONIGHT<br>(Int - Bamville Club - Night) | 58 |
| 93A | HEADLIGHTS<br>(Ext - Street - Night) | 61 |
| 94 | DIXIE/VERA IN KITCHEN<br>(Int - Dwyer Apt. - Night) | 61 |
| 95 | VERA UNDRESSING<br>(Int - Dixie's Bedroom - Night) | 61 |
| 96 | DIXIE SAYS HE'S QUITTING<br>(Int - Dixie's Bedroom - Night) | 62 |
| 98 | NOT REAL LIFE - IT'S JAZZ<br>(Int - Dixie's Bedroom - Night) | 63 |
| 97 | TEA & TOAST WITH PSYCHOPATH<br>(Int - Dixie's Bedroom - Night) | 64 |
| A77 | DUTCH HAS NEW SUIT<br>(Int - Dutch's Apt. Lobby - Day) | 64 |
| B77 | DIXIE BREAKS WITH DUTCH<br>(Ext - Dutch's Apt. - Day) | 65 |
| 77 | STORMY WEATHER<br>(Int - Cotton Club - Night) | 66 |

| Sc. #/Sc. | | Page # |
|---|---|---|
| 78 | DEPRESSION/NUMBERS MONTAGE | 66a |
| 81 | ILL WIND<br>(Int - Cotton Club - Night) | 67 |
| 85 | JEWETT OFFERS GUNS<br>(Int - Numbers Bank - Day) | 67 |
| 135A | ABBA FIXES 527<br>(Int - Office - Day) | 67 |
| 80 | NUMBERS WAR MONTAGE<br>(Ext - Harlem - Day) | 67 |
| 127C | SANDMAN & LILA AFTER SHOW<br>(Int - Backstage - Night) | 68 |
| 99 | VINCE WRECKS BAMVILLE<br>(Int - Bamville Club - Night) | 68 |
| 127D | SANDMAN & LILA IN KITCHEN<br>(Int - Kitchen - Night) | 69 |
| 80B | 527 NEWSPAPER HEADLINES | 69 |
| 84 | NUMBERS BANKERS MEETING (527 HITS)<br>(Int - Numbers Bank - Day) | 69 |
| 127E | LILA ROSE QUITS<br>(Int - Backstage - Night) | 70 |
| 135 | STAY BLUE AND DIE<br>(Int - Black Speakeasy - Night) | 70 |
| 105 | SANDMAN/LILA OUTSIDE VERA'S<br>(Ext - Vera's Club - Night) | 71 |
| 103 | VERA'S CLUB CELEBRATION<br>(Int - Vera's Club - Night) | 72 |
| 103A | VINCE BREAKS WITH DUTCH<br>(Int - Back Hall of Club - Night) | 73 |
| 104 | DUTCH SEES DIXIE/VERA IN LOVE<br>(Int - Vera's Club - Night) | 74 |
| 113 | SANDMAN/LILA REGISTER<br>(Int - Hotel Register - Night) | 75 |

| Sc. #/Sc. | | Page # |
|---|---|---|
| 114 | SANDMAN/LILA LOVE SCENE<br>(Int - Hotel Room - Night) | 75 |
| 107A | SHAKE<br>(Ext - Alley - Night) | 76 |
| 115 | BURN THAT JEW<br>(Ext - Street - Day) | 77 |
| 116 | BABY KILLING<br>(Ext - Street - Day) | 77 |
| 117 | HEADLINES ON BABY KILLING | 77 |
| 117A | FRENCHY GETS MESSAGE<br>(Int - C.C. Backstage - Night) | 77 |
| 117B | FRENCHY KIDNAPPING<br>(Ext - Cotton Club - Night) | 78 |
| 117C | FRENCHY IN CAR<br>(Int - Vince's Car - Night) | 78 |
| 117D | VERA SEES DIXIE IN BAMVILLE<br>(Int - Bamville - Night) | 79 |
| X117 | VERA WARNS DIXIE<br>(Ext - Bamville - Night) | 79 |
| 117E | MADDEN & DIXIE IN LIMO<br>(Int - Limousine - Night) | 80 |
| X118 | VINCE LOOKS OUT WINDOW<br>(Int - Cheap Hotel - Day) | 81 |
| 118 | DIXIE RANSOMS FRENCHY<br>(Int - Cheap Hotel - Day) | 82 |
| 118C | FRENCHY GIVES WATCH<br>(Int - Madden's Office - Night) | 84 |
| X118 | SANDMAN/CLAY REUNION<br>(Int - Bamville - Night) | 85 |
| 118C | FRENCHY GIVES WATCH<br>(Int - Madden's Office - Night) | 86 |
| 118A | VINCE ENTERS DRUGSTORE<br>(Ext - Drugstore - Night) | 87 |

| Sc. #/Sc. | | Page # |
|---|---|---|
| 118D | VINCE KILLED IN DRUGSTORE  (Int - Drugstore - Night) | 88 |
| 118F | MADDEN HANGS UP PHONE  (Int - Madden's Office - Night) | 88 |
| 118G | ENTERTAINMENT HEADLINES | 88 |

## 140-177  COTTON CLUB II

| 140 | Minnie the Moocher | 88 |
|---|---|---|
| 141 | Lila passes with Chaplin | 89 |
| 141A | Winnie late for show | 89 |
| 142 | Everybody seated | 89 |
| 143 | Winnie, Sandman backstage | 90 |
| 144 | Doin' New Low Down | 90 |
| 145 | Lady with Fan, Luciano booth | 90 |
| 146 | Dutch phone | 91 |
| 147 | Bumpy and Mike Best | 92 |
| 146 | Dutch tells Vera to disappear | 93 |
| 146A | First dark girl | 94 |
| 150 | Frances up stairs | 94 |
| 149 | Frances causes a scene | 94 |
| 152 | Dixie/Vera curtains | 98 |
| 153 | Dixie/Dutch confrontation | 99 |
| 153A | Gun lands by Holmes | 103 |
| 154 | Dutch and Abba fight down stairs | 103 |
| 155 | Stark restores order | 103 |
| 155A | Dutch and gang into car | 103 |
| 154B | Luciano to phone | 103 |
| A156 | Conspire in car | 103 |
| 155B | A Cappella Tap | 104 |
| 157 | Luciano gets wine | 104 |
| 156 | Dutch at chop house | 104 |
| 156A | Luciano pops cork | 105 |
| 158B | Abba killed | 105 |
| 159 | Dutch killed | 105 |
| 160 | Luciano makes toast | 105 |
| 164 | Lila leaves table | 105 |
| 165 | Sandman/Lila backstage | 105 |
| 163 | Dixie meets Luciano | 106 |
| 166 | Chaplin table | 107 |
| 166A | Dixie/Vera farewell | 107 |
| 167 | Daybreak Express | 109 |
| 168-173 | Grand Central Station | 109 |
| 174 | Company bows | 110 |